From the Projects to the Pulpit:

From Pain, to Purpose, to Destiny

From the Projects to the Pulpit:

From Pain, to Purpose, to Destiny

Hurricane Katrina

This is a work of non-fiction. The events and persons described and discussed within are real. However, names have been changed or omitted to protect identities. The opinions expressed in this book are solely the perceptions of the author and do not represent the opinions or thoughts of the publisher.

Published by CLF Publishing, LLC. 3281 E. Guasti Rd. Seventh Floor. Ontario, CA 91761.

Edited by Dr. C. White-Elliott in the voice and diction of Katrina May.

Cover design created by Senir Design, Inc. For more information, please write to info@senirdesign.com.

ISBN # 978-0-9857372-3-8

Printed in the United States of America.

DEDICATION

I would like to give a special thank you, appreciation and dedication to You, my Abba Father, my Alpha and Omega, my Beginning and my Ending, my Jehovah Jirah, my Great Provider, my Jehovah Nissi, you are my Victory, you are my Jehovah Shalom, my Peace, Jehovah Rafah, my Healer; you are all of the above and so much more to me. You knew me when I was only a spirit. Before you even put me in my mother's womb, you knew me. You know everything about me, and I thank you. I thank you for everything that you allowed me to go through and everything that you will allow me to ever go through. Thank you for all that you have done and for all that you will ever do. Thank you for sharing your greatest love from heaven up above. And through His love, I'm able to love. I thank you for creating me just the way you've done. Now, I'm able to appreciate your Glorious Son. You have been the rock that I have leaned on. To this day, I am now standing on you because I know that it's only through you that will lift me and strengthen me to do all that I do. Thank you for being you. Thank you allowing me to enter in your presence like never before. Thank you for your wonderful miraculous glory. It's only through you that I'm able to tell my story.

ACKNOWLEDGEMENTS

Special thanks are also given to Pastor Charles and Rosalind Travis who have both been such an inspiration to me. I thank you for going up and above being my pastors. I bless God for you. Words really can't explain all I would like to say about how much of an impact you've been in my life and my children's lives as well. When I first came to your ministry, I knew I had a few issues, but I realized I had a long way to go. God has been so good to me in your ministry; you fed me well, you taught me well, and you disciplined me well. I learned accountability, structure, servitude, and lots of humility. You poured so much into me, and I am grateful for you. I pray that for every seed you've sown into my life, you will reap one hundred fold. I speak health and wealth over your life and your ministry. Every seed sown into my children and me will not be in vain, for some plant and others water, but God adds the increase, and I'm expecting a great increase for us all in Jesus' name.

TABLE OF CONTENTS

Introduction

I am sharing my life story about how I became a survivor of hurt, pain, and betrayal in the hood of South Central, the projects and the church house. My story will help all those who feel like they were the only ones in the world who have been through certain things. I believe some of the things that I have gone through will help those that have been through some of the same things. There are so many people that have put their life experiences in a closet and locked the door and haven't been healed or delivered. They haven't even begun to touch the surface of the matter, but they put on their make up or their mask and even their camouflage and just exist like nothing ever happened.

I am sharing my story to help those that need and want help and want to get out of certain situations. Maybe you have never experienced being raped or molested or physical, mental, verbal or spiritual abuse. Well, after reading my story, there is a great chance you won't be. But if by any chance you do, there is ammunition inside my story to help you get healed and delivered much sooner than I did. It took me forty years to be healed and delivered. I believe my life story will provide you with a shortcut out of Egypt and out of bondage. I found out that the children of Israel were in bondage, and that they had taken a journey for forty years that could have been completed so much sooner. I believe that a person doesn't always have to learn from experience. One is much wiser to learn from someone else's experience. The bible says to be wise as a serpent and humble as a dove. I also believe that an ounce of prevention is worth more than a pound of cure any day.

Chapter One

From Riches to Rags:

The Seed was Planted

I never thought it would have taken my mother's diagnosis with Cancer to get me at a place where I was quiet enough to hear God say, "It's time now. Start writing." There I was sitting at my mom's bedside not knowing if she was going to make it or not. She was struggling with Lung Cancer, and at the time, it seemed so serious. She was hooked up to all these tubs and machines, and so many things came to me. But, one thing stood out the most, and I said to myself *you can't die now. I have too many things I haven't told you. I have so much I need to tell you.*

I know it seems kind of selfish, but it was the way I felt. There were things that I needed to let her know that happened to me that I was holding her partly responsible for. I needed to forgive her, and there were some things I needed forgiveness for as well. At that time, the Lord said, "Start writing now," so I took my notebook out of my bible bag, and I began to write.

If you don't mind, I would be honored if you would go with me as I take a journey back down memory lane.

It all started when my little fast-tail mom was hanging out of her project window watching my dad-to-be. She yelled, "Hey, what's your name? Are you going to the liquor store? Can you bring me a bottle of ??" And she threw her money down to him out the window, and the rest is a story to be told.

At the time, she was only about twelve or thirteen years old, and he was about seventeen or eighteen. She had a crush on my dad, but he was a little too old for her. A little while later, his parents sent him back to Louisiana to attend Louisiana State University (LSU). He went there for two years or more. That is, until the school made him mad and he decided to take it out on himself by dropping out of school and moving back to Cali.

I believe my dad always had some issues, especially when it came to his dad. I think he held a lot against him for not spending the appropriate time with him and leaving his mom to raise him and his siblings alone. So anyway, he returned back on the set in the projects, and he was known for being Mr. Bad, and he was very popular.

He met up with my mom and married her when she was sixteen, and they had my big sister shortly after (if you know what I mean).

And then I came two and a half years later. My dad wanted a boy so badly that my name was going to be Robert the III. It was such a mess; my parents were so wild that they didn't even have a name for me at the hospital. My birth certificate read Baby Girl Taylor. That's crazy; I know. For as far back as I can remember, everyone has always said that I was a bad little girl, and some would call me a bad seed. But allow me to tell you my side of the story.

My sister and I barely wanted to go over to the ghetto to visit my grandma, and I loved my grandma and I still do. But that didn't have much to do with the way her children would act and treat us. I thought they were raised like animals.

First of all, they would cuss and fight like they were fighting someone on the streets. They would literally fight for their lives, with butcher knives. They would hit each other in the face with bottles, irons and skillets, whatever they could get their hands on, other than a pistol. It was sad. I didn't know where it came from because my grandma wasn't violent, but I guess she didn't play though. Where I came from was completely different. I was raised in the suburbs, in a whole other atmosphere. I went to the best schools and lived in the same building with the celebrities, such as Dennis the Menace, Mike Mitchell, the pitcher for the Dodgers, and the Dozier Family just to name a few. Not only did I live by them, but I was actually close friends with their children.

We had a maid and nanny who took care of us most of the time and taught us a lot of things that we needed to know. Other times, the nanny's boyfriend would come over and bring us awesome jelly donuts, and they would smoke pot and eat the jelly donuts. They gave us some of both. I later found out that they only gave us the herb to put us to sleep, so they could handle their business. I wasn't any older than about seven, and I was something else. My nanny was too. I remember one specific day at the hair salon. She took us to our regular bi-weekly hair appointment, and I was just sitting there. I heard her tell our stylist to give us perms.

It wasn't much that got by me even as a child, so I told her not to have a perm put in our hair. My dad said no perms, and my sister, who was older than I was, used wisdom and didn't say anything. As I look back, she probably wanted a straight silky perm thinking her hair was going to grow long and straight like the white girls. No disrespect, but a compliment to the white girls. As my nanny put me in the chair, the stylist grabbed the perm to put it in my hair. I cut up, started jerking, moving, and acting up. My nanny slapped me, and all I could do was grab my face and cry. I told her, "My daddy gone get you. I'm telling my daddy." That was it for our nanny.

As I look back on that event and others in my childhood, I realize I was quite mannish. I remember one night, we had company over, and my mom and dad were having intercourse, and the people were peaking or doing something at the door. I did it too. I believe I went further and cracked the door or looked through the peephole. That was my first lustful, perverted act. The door of perversion was opened at six years old; then, a couple of years later, my sister and I would lie on our hands and grind. Then she said, "Let's try this thing out of the fish tank." It would vibrate, and it really hit our spot. That's what we would call it- hitting our spot.

As time moved on, I was about nine, and I was humping with my younger uncle. He was a year younger than I was, but he was grown in spirit and aggressive. I humped my cousins too. I even humped my best friend. That was weird and awkward; it was our first and last time doing that, and we said we wouldn't ever do it or ever tell it, so I'm breaking our word that we gave each other, but it's for the good if it can help someone.

I would say that I was the hump master. That and kissing were all I knew. As time went on, the boys would try to get some- like sticking something, but it wasn't going down. I just didn't play that. But they were good for a grind anytime. The older I got, I saw my sister and my cousin taking turns with my uncle on my dad's side. Then I said, "Do me. I want to do it too." He rubbed himself against me. There was no way I could handle the real deal inside, but I do believe he did it to my cousin. I asked my cousin when we became adults if our uncle had done anything to her, and she said he did try, but she didn't want to talk about it.

The next person who violated me was on my mom's side of the family. My mom's cousin pulled his stuff out when we were watching TV on the floor. First of all, I had no business sitting there with him. There were about five people in the bed ahead of us, including my aunty and nobody knew anything. He proceeded to fondle me, and I hit my spot. I must be honest, he was a grown man, and he knew exactly how to touch a young girl to make her feel good. I just knew that it was all my fault. I would always feel so nasty and bad afterwards. I got up and went and lay on the couch. He brought his nasty, perverted self in there and tried to lay on me. He wanted to put his stuff in mine, but it wasn't going down. I must have pushed him right on the floor and said, "Get off, and don't ever try that again." He left me alone, and I never told anyone.

Then in broad daylight, one of my mom's friends saw me sitting on the couch and began talking to me. He went for it right in my grandma's living room. That house was a busy house, but no one came in. That's crazy.

I can't recall being fast and wearing tight clothes or anything. I was more like a tomboy, but look at what was going on with me. I also remember one night when my mom and dad had a fight. When they fought, most of the time, I would go with my dad. I was about seven or eight years old, and he took me with him. I really loved my dad, and he was really fond of me, but there was one particular night that I will always remember. It was the way he laid me down on the couch at my auntie's house. He was so delicate with me. He touched me with a certain touch of love that made me think he was going to have me, but he kissed me on my forehead and went to another part of the house. That night has always been in my mind.

There are a lot of things that I have forgotten, but I never forgot that. I believe I didn't know how to distance the love from a daughter and father because my dad was very affectionate with me, but he never touched me improperly. But, I held so much against my dad because he was a well-respected man who went for bad, and he had paid and bought several people. How could he allow someone to touch his little princess? The older I became, the more confusing it became because my dad loved on me, and that's the way you expect a guy to treat you and no less.

At the same time, my dad abused me verbally, physically, and emotionally. I didn't know how to feel. I loved my dad, but another part of me hated him. At times, he abused my sister and my mom, so it was like living with Dr. Jekyll and Mr. Hyde. When it was good, it was good, and when it was bad, it was bad. I believe growing up, the bad outweighed the good. I know that's because some of the decisions that I made. I remember having to have myself prayed up in order to go around him or my family because whenever I would go to see my mom, he was there and found a reason to act up. When I went to visit my sister, he would come there and cut up too. Finally, I found myself allowing six months to go by without seeing him, but I knew that it was a problem.

The problem was also in me because as a woman of God and an evangelist, how could I deal with all types of people and their mess but not deal with the demands of my dad. Finally, I began to go and see him. He would trip out, so it would be a while before I went again but I did not stay away as long as I did before. I would pray and speak to God, and God said that my dad needed to be saved too and that I am the bible that my dad will read, so I began to deal with him differently. You see, God told me that love covers a multitude of sin and to just love on him and not to fight fire with fire. The fire can be put out with lots of love.

Another confusing and disappointing thing was, while my sister and I were growing up, he would call my mom, my sister and me very bad names. It was just something about that "b" word. Later, when I got saved, he really didn't understand it, but he wouldn't use the "b" word as much. One night, he sat at the end of my bed in my house and told me that he was my god. I told him, "No, you are not," but he always wanted to be over us. He wanted to have complete control over our minds. When I told him he wasn't my god, he told me I must be out of my mother's you-know-what, and I politely dialed 911 and asked the police to escort him out. He was hurt and hot, but he was not my God.

My dad was so good to everybody else, but when it came to us, he was hard. I know now that was to make us strong, but I could have done without all the abuse. The verbal abuse did more damage than anything, and the physical abuse set me right up to take even more abuse from other men. Not only did I have to go through all of the abuse from my dad, but the boys and men also abused my body.

When my mom and dad separated, my dad took my sister and me and dropped us off at my grandma's house to live. My sister and I suffered when they separated. We were forced to live completely different lives. I loved my mom, but I was a daddy's girl. No doubt about it. I just knew that he wasn't leaving me there. Can you imagine being snatched out of your comfort zone? My grandma had fourteen kids (seven boys and seven girls), and most of them were on drugs and alcohol; they were gangbangers, pimps, and hustlers. We were living like animals on Fifty-Seventh Street at my grandmother's house. Most of the time, we had to fend for ourselves. We had plenty of hungry days. We had to hustle up ramen noodles, hot links and a dollar's worth of lunchmeat. Sometimes, the grownups would try and take our food. They took our money; they stole out of our panties if the money was there. I really don't know where my mom was at that time. I remember waking up really early one morning with my grandma cooking breakfast and singing spiritual songs. She went under her China cabinet and got a bottle of Courvoisier. She poured a nip in her coffee. I was also drinking coffee with her and asked her for some as well. She gave me what I asked for. I was only six years old. That was the beginning of a hard addiction and struggle in my life.

Sad to say, when I had my daughters, I left them in the same hell house. I just couldn't believe that I repeated the past. I actually blocked out the event of my experiences, until a couple of years ago when I had it out with my oldest daughter. She told me what I had done. She said every night when she and her sisters would go to sleep, she slept with both of her legs across their bodies so that no one could touch them. I don't know how she knew something because I had never told her. As a matter of fact, it cut me to the core when she told me that because somewhere in my life I blocked out all the stuff I went through over there, and I turned around and subjected my daughters to the same environment. I thank God nothing happened to them - at least not there.

As life went on, I allowed my daughters to be put in other compromising situations over the years. That thing is a generational curse. It comes to destroy lives.

Let's get back to the story of my childhood. I remember one time my little uncle had the audacity to take me in the back alley in a shack and told me to suck his stuff. I said no, but he was a real bad act. He used to beat me up all the time, but I told him no anyway. He was really intimidating. The details of all that happened are a little blurry. But I believe I was on my knees, and I began to do it. But, I just couldn't stomach it, so I jumped up and ran out. That was so degrading for my own uncle to do me like that.

I was about twelve years old then, and the longer I stayed, the more it would happen. In spite of it all, God kept me. He never allowed one of those men to penetrate me. They were being used by the enemy, and they imparted a lustful and perverted spirit and a masturbation spirit, which is a cold spirit, into me. It was planted so deep that it *was* the penetrating. It has been there so long, so the more I did it, the more it grew. I was about eight or nine when I started, so that thing grew in me. As I grew, it grew.

As an adult, when I got saved and was celibate, I would find myself relieving myself in that manner. But it only took me backwards. It became a stronghold and a strong man in my life. I would find myself going years without doing it, but if I didn't watch my gates, I would get caught up. I have to guard my eye gates. I can't watch sex scenes in movies. I guard my ear gates from sexual conversations. I even must guard my hands. I have to be careful about everything. It could happen even today if I'm not prayed up and if I allow my gates to be contaminated with filth, meaning open doors to sexual perversion.

If it happened to me, it could happen to anyone. It didn't happen to me to destroy me, but God has used it as a vehicle to help several people, young and old. When I share my testimony, I tell mothers to watch their daughters and their sons too. I tell fathers to protect their family. There is so much more to raising children than just whipping and punishing. It's been said that spirits have attacked every family. Let me set the record straight. It is a spirit, and it has no respect of persons. It comes to kill, steal and destroy. So, I have to pray that I don't fall in divers temptation because that thing has been the thorn in my side.

I feel like the apostle Paul when he asked if God would just move the thorn from his side and the Lord told him, "That's what keeps you before me." Paul also said every time he tries to do good, evil presents itself. He said when I want to do good, bad is present. He said, "The things I ought not to do, I find myself doing them." So, I press towards the mark of the high calling. I speak a healing, deliverance and press in your spirit, in Jesus' name.

Chapter Two

All My Life I had to Fight

At the age of thirteen, I went to Edison Jr. High. I thought I was the baddest thing there, but all bad people have their day. One day while I was at school, a girl named Charla, who was the bully of the school, came up and cut me in the lunch line. I never played when it came to my food, so I politely walked right back in front of her. She did it again, and I went back in front of her. Then, she snatched me and started slinging me all around the whole lunch area, cleaning the tables with my body.

I was about one hundred and twenty pounds, and she weighed about three hundred pounds. I remembered what my grandmother taught us in self defense: if you fight a big person, don't let her get up on you. When I got loose, I started lightening her face up like a Christmas tree. She caught hold to me, and she slung me and threw me like a rag doll. I ran right back on her. I never gave up, and everybody said that she was going to get me after school. When she caught up with me, yea I was scared, but I didn't let her know. She said I had heart, and I hit hard too, but I was cool. We became cool from that point on.

She really turned out to be cool. Sad to say, as we got a little older, she got hooked up with the wrong boy. He was one of the finest and most popular boys in the neighborhood, and I believe she fell in love with him. He and his friends pulled a train on her over by Compton Park, but don't quote me on that. She pretty much lost her mind and was never the same.

Later, there was another bully, a long-term bully who turned out to be a frienemy. That's short for a friend and an enemy. Our first time meeting was in the lunch area. My friends from elementary and I were at our table. Two of my friends happened to have a ghetto cousin straight out the projects. She came walking up to our table. I was 'all that' in school, so I stuck out like a sore thumb. Unfortunately, she was talking to her cousin and looked at me and said, "Who is this 'b'?" I think she wanted to sit down or something, but she really wasn't welcome. She very politely took a napkin off the table and put it on top of my coffee cake and smashed it. Yea, my coffee cake! They were good back then, and they still are. I don't know what it was with me, but I didn't play when it came to my food. So you know a fight was about to begin, but her cousins that were there begged both of us not to fight. I had already beaten both of them up in elementary. At that point, I knew I would have a fight on my hands.

Later, I started going out with Crystal's brother, and she liked it. But every chance she got, she was hating and wanting to fight because she was one that always went for bad. I remember one day when her brother was kind of mad at me, not real mad, but he just wanted a little entertainment. Looking back, I know what that was now. He would sick his sister on me for my necklace that he had given me. He told her that if she could get it off my neck that she could have it. She attacked me like a mad lady, but you know I had to handle my business. Then, he began to help her and his brother and my cousin came to rescue me. Good lookin'.

I'm just sharing how I had to fight all my life. Another fight in the lunch area was with some girls from the other side that did not like me or my crew. I believe we had gone up to their park on the other side of the tracks and met their guys in their neighborhood, so they started tripping out on us. So, you know we had to handle our business. Usually, it was my best friend Almond who would defend and fight for me. But this particular time, I tried to protect and fight for her, but she wasn't having it. She fought her own battles, no matter how beautiful she was. Almond was beautiful with the most beautiful black skin, long, thick, wavy, black silky hair, and a bad Coca-Cola shape to go with it. So, me and another girl began to fight, but I really didn't get a chance to finish. Almond said, "Move. I got this." She wore her out. They were not expecting that.

The following week, I was slipping, not even tripping, and they got to crippin'. I was in the lunch line, and I ran right smack in the middle of the two cousins. I was almost to the front of the line, and she turned around and fired on me. We started locking up, and I started beating. I started feeling someone hitting me from the back bam, bam, bam. All I could do was think about when my granny would say if you're fighting and somebody jumps in, you make sure you focus on the main one you're fighting. That's what I did because I couldn't move forward or backwards. I was locked in between those bars that separate the lines. I was wearing out the one in the front, and the one behind me was wearing the back of my head out.

My girl Almond couldn't get to me once she found out it was me that was fighting. My aunty Yogi worked her little black skinny self up there, and she got the girl off my back. Boy, did I feel the ease, but not too much longer. Our principle came, and Aunty Yogi was so wild and fast that she swung and hit him. He yelled out, "Who hit me?" He suspended everybody but Aunty Yogi. That was my first and I believe my last time getting suspended. And I got worn out when my dad found out. My mom, on the other hand, never whooped me, except once in my life, and she wasn't able to do it then.

That particular time was one day when we got our allowance. My mom said, "Don't spend all of your money." My sister and I went shopping with our aunty to a new store on Central Avenue. They had socks, panties, barrettes, and all types of cute little stuff. We bought some bubble gum tennis shoes. Some people call them girlies. When we got home, my mom asked us, "How much money did you spend?" We had spent it all. My mom was furious. We had a new little sister, but I didn't care too much for her because I was my mommy's baby. Actually, when my mom was pregnant, we were close. I loved her buttermilk cornbread, but I felt like Esau when he sold his birthright for beans. Check the story out in the book of Genesis.

I would rub my mother's stomach, but when she went to the hospital and came home with a baby, I said, "Where did she come from and where is she going?" I was like Martin Lawrence: She got to get up out of here.

Back to when we got home from shopping, my mom decided that she was going to whoop us. The oldest would always go first, so she took my sister to the back and started whooping her. Then it came to my turn, and she came to get me and took me to the back room. As soon as she raised the belt to hit me, we heard a loud sound and a loud cry that followed. It was my little sister. My mom dropped the belt and ran and got the baby. She was cool with me at that point.

At that time, we had everything that I could imagine that I wanted. I was such a brat. Every year when my sister's birthday came around, my parents had to have a gift for me also or I would throw a fit. When my sister turned thirteen, they gave her her first diamond ring and gave me a little red robe. I cried and did not understand that at all. There I was ruining my big sister's shine, but I didn't know then what I was doing. She has let me know by now over the years how she was completely responsible for me. Anything I thought about doing wrong, she got in trouble.

One day when I was about seven years old, I had a nickel or a dime and was waiting for the ice cream truck. I ran into the street, and my sister grabbed my hand. She went instead. Out of nowhere, a station wagon came and hit my sister. She flew up in the air, hit the ground, and blacked out. The next time I saw my sister, she was laid up in the hospital in a body cast. She had to keep a cast on for almost a year, but I didn't even know she went through all of that for me until later in life. I felt so sad and sorry for her.

While I was attending Edison Jr. High, I met a boy. I liked the boys on my street and in my neighborhood, but it was something about this boy. He had a certain charm and was a mac out of this world. He wound up in my PE class, and he complimented me all the time on my lady of the night legs.

That's crazy. I know. When I was growing up, I always wanted to be a call girl traveling and living a rich and exciting life. But I beg to differ now. I went to my friend's thirteenth birthday party, and he was there. We danced to one of my favorite songs *Always and Forever*, and when he dipped me on the high note, I thought I fell in love. Then, I found out he was a project boy, and I liked the project boys. It was just something about them. It was the rough lifestyle and the hard core life I guess because he didn't have anything to offer.

I don't even remember him ever taking me to a movie. But I was in love. I had already been to the projects with my best friend. We were going with these other boys, and one in particular was my boy. But baby, I shot him to the curb when I met the new one. But he didn't miss me one bit at that time because he was such a player from the Himalaya. As time went on, I held on to my virginity for what it was worth. To me, it meant a lot. I just was not about to let nobody stick nothing in me. We started going out. It wasn't no time before he was asking to get between my legs, and I said, "No, it isn't happening." We could kiss and grind, but not the real thing. He said okay, and we stayed together for about two years.

My friends and I would have sleepovers. By that time, my mom had moved to the projects, and I had friends who would spend the night over my house, and I would spend the night at theirs. I was close friends with his sister for what that was worth because we fought more than anything.

When we had sleepovers, we would talk about who was a virgin and who wasn't. At first, we all were, but suddenly my girls started giving up their goods, and I was about the last one. They were talking about losing their virginity didn't really hurt, especially his little fast sister. She was younger than I was, and I let them peer pressure me into giving it up.

One day my family went to Magic Mountain, and I told them I wasn't feeling well and that I wanted to stay home. Yea right! What kid turns down Magic Mountain? That was a warning sign right there for my parents, but they didn't catch it. I planned that day to the "T." I told him we could do it that night because not only did I have my girls sweating me, but he was really sweating me by then. He was talking about dumping me because his boys were getting some and he wasn't. So he was going to go with the girls that were giving it up. When I decided to go for it, I was fifteen years old.

He came over, and we began to try it. My cousin and my dad's best friend were knocking at my door. We were busted. So, I told him to get his shoes and jump out the window. My room was upstairs. As he hesitated, I pushed him out. The second time we tried, he came over, and we were on my couch. At one time, we tried, but it didn't work because I was asking if he knew what he was doing. He told me to just tell him if it hurt and he would stop. Yea right! He didn't know what he was doing. He got on top of me and thought he could just ram it in. I almost shot to the ceiling. I made him stop, and I didn't try it for a long time.

Everybody used to go over to their next door neighbor's house and play grown up. Finally, he got me over there, and we were in the bed. It went down, and yes, it hurt really badly. I didn't enjoy it at all. As a matter of fact, for the record, I didn't reach an organism until I was twenty-five. No hard feelings to those within those ten years. I don't mean to hurt your manhood, but I got to keep it real since this is my life story.

Back to the supposed special night that turned into a nightmare. When we had done it, evidently he had popped my cherry, and I bled. I jumped up and left. When I went home, there was a little blood in my underwear. I thought that was from the pain and everything that had just happened. The next day, I went over to my boyfriend's house. He dumped me and said, "You nasty. I don't want you." I said, "What did I do?" I thought it was because I finally gave him some, and he didn't have respect for me. But he said, "You did it to me on your monthly, and it was blood on the lady's sheets." I didn't know; I was new to the sex game. I just knew that I didn't do any mess like that and the lady should have known it, but I believe she wanted him for herself anyway. The news spread all around the projects. How embarrassing! I always did know how to pick them.

As time went on, the break up didn't last long. We got back together. I looked up the next month, and my mother nature didn't come. I had to tell him I was pregnant. Do you know that dirty dog told me, "It isn't mine." That is a famous line. Remember, I was a virgin, and it was my first and last time for a while.

When my dad found out I was pregnant, he nearly had a heart attack. We were no longer living in the projects. We had moved back to Fifty-Seventh Street. My dad made an appointment for me to go to the doctor to get an abortion. He planned to pick me up at seven o'clock. At six, I heard someone at my grandma's back door. I saw a green station wagon in the alley. My boyfriend's older sister was driving. His brother was the look out. My boyfriend came to the door to get me, and at that point my whole life was at my grandma's back door. The only thing that ran through my mind was *Do I go or do I stay and go with my dad and allow him to force me to kill my baby?* I jumped into the car and went to the projects. It was a journey, and I did not know what I was in for.

Chapter Three

Run Away Child, Running Wild

When I ran away from home, my dad would get on my sister. He would blame her for what was going on with me. There were several times and days that she came looking for me. I would look in her eyes, and I knew that she couldn't go home without me. I preferred to suffer the consequences and go home with her, so she didn't have to suffer. But when I suffered, she suffered. There were also times when I just wasn't going back home, but if my sister came for me, I went. I would always take the chance of getting caught by letting her know where I was and how I was because I remember she told me one time, and one time only, that she would be so worried about me because she didn't know if I was dead or alive. So, I gave her my word that I would always let her know of my well being. I would tell my homegirls to bring my sister to me wherever I was because we have a bond that is unbreakable.

There were times when my crazy dad would come looking for me. At least, I thought he was crazy, but I differ now. My friends would hide me, but I would call them frienemies (a friend and enemy). My dad wanted what was best for me, and my frienemies wanted the best out of me. Let me give a special shot out to my dad right here and right now. Thank you, Daddy for every time you just couldn't sleep when your baby girl was out there in this great big world. I didn't understand it then, but from great experience and pain, I understand now. Thank you for not giving up on me. You had such great expectations for me. I will reach not only your expectations, but I will reach my Heavenly Father's expectations as well.

I was about fourteen when I started selling drugs, and I was about seventeen when I started using them. I enjoyed doing both: using and selling. It was nothing like smoking a primo joint. Some would call them lace joints. When I would roll one up and smoke it, I would be in a whole other place. I saw where it was eating up my profits.

I remember a person told me when I started dealing drugs to make sure I didn't get high on my own supplies, but I wound up being my best customer.

Even though I was pregnant, I continued to hang out and sell drugs because I was raised with a certain life style and allowance. I had to have money, so I had to get it. My boyfriend was weak and on drugs.

He was only eighteen himself, so he sure couldn't help me out. He barely could help himself. I remember being in a cold place where the people that I was staying with wanted all my little money and food stamps so I had to sell drugs to survive. I remember thinking I wish I didn't make the mistakes that I had made. I wished I could go to sleep and wake up and my old life with my mommy and daddy would be back, but it never happened. So I had to deal with it and make the best out of a cold situation.

I had plenty of cold nights on the porches of the gang violence and drug-infested streets trying to make a dollar out of fifteen cents, but it made no sense at all. I even remember falling asleep outside. You see, the very people that seemed so cool in the beginning didn't turn out to be so cool after all. If I didn't march to their beat, they would dog me out and tell me to get out of their house and you can't eat this and you can't eat that. Not to mention the guy that I ran away to be with. It was like I wasn't with him since I ran away, only when he wanted to lie with me. During the day, he would be with other girls, and it wasn't too much I could do because I was stuck and couldn't go home. At least, I thought I couldn't, so I hung in there.

As time passed by slowly, I was getting bigger and bigger. It was so much fun. My body had completely changed. I went to my prenatal care, but the dad never did. His mom would support me sometimes when I needed someone to go with me or when I had false labor. I was ready to have the baby, but she wasn't ready.

A couple of weeks later, it was time. My water broke, and my friend's sister Nancy took me to the hospital, and I just knew she was going to leave me and just drop me off. The Lord knew I was scared. Thank you so much for your support to a young broken lonely girl like me. That meant the world to me at the time. The hospital that my doctor sent me to was Queen of Mary's Hospital, which was a nuns' hospital. There I was only fifteen with no husband, no baby's dad, and not even my mom. I was horrified.

It came time for the nurse to check me, and I told her that she was hurting me. She replied. "It didn't hurt when you were doing what you were doing. And by the way, if you're going to have this baby here, I need to examine you." She was a heavy-set mean nurse with big hands. I had only had intercourse that one time, so I started to cry. I told her to give me a skinny nurse. Then she said, "I don't have to take this." She walked out and a skinny nice nurse came in, and everything was fine besides the fourteen hours of labor that I had to go through. My baby was seven pounds and two ounces.

My dad found out and picked me up from the hospital and brought me all kinds of oil for my skin and things for the baby, and it worked as well as expected. Then, my aunty said for me and the baby to come live with her. By the way, it was a girl, and she gave me a run for my fun. When I said I thought it would be fun to bathe and dress her up and stuff like that, nobody ever told me how babies cry. My favorite doll was a Baby Alive, but I had complete control over her. I did not have that kind of control over my real baby.

My aunties said when you feed them and clean them, they would be fine. Well, I did it all, and she still cried. I didn't know what to do, and my aunt didn't come in and help at all. My baby cried so much that all I could do was cry right along with her. Then my life saver came in and picked her up and took her in the room with him and my aunt, and all I heard was silence. It seems like I can still hear her crying, but that was almost thirty years ago.

So I made it through that but not without battle wounds. I could not believe how I had all those black snake-looking things all over my stomach, my breast, my back and my butt. I was devastated about what had happened to my smooth beautiful tender body. Yes, I still have the black snake-looking things, and they are called stretch marks. I was too young for my body to stretch like that, and that's why the stretch marks came.

When the baby turned six weeks old, I took her back to where she was conceived. To this day, I wish I hadn't. Her daddy was high, and his homeboys said he had a whack attack. I didn't know about him doing that stuff. I was so ashamed, and I felt sorry that he was my baby's dad, but I dealt with it. I left and went back to my aunt's house, but I believe she gave me a curfew, and I didn't follow it. So, I thought it was best to leave.

I went back to the projects, and I had to lay up with full grown men. When I was in the projects, I really went through some stuff. But, I was too scared to go back home, so I went through all types of things. Papa's family began to treat me bad at Ms C's house. At first, it was all good, but once they felt like I was trapped, they started treating me pretty bad. So, I moved next door to one of my friend's sister's house (Ms. Karen). She had a nice house, and she dressed nicely, or I would say past nice. Back in the day, I liked 'hot mama' clothes. To each its own.

I didn't know what she really had going on. It turned out that she was a hooker, and she would set me up with grown men to get money from them. I was only about seventeen, and I remember having to allow men to have sex with me, so that I could have somewhere to sleep. Everybody thought she was trying to turn me out and maybe she was, but I just wasn't the type to have a lot of sex with just anybody. I know it's because of what I went through when I was molested. I felt so dirty, and I looked at all older men that tried to talk to me as dirty nasty old men.

So when I left Ms. Karen's house, Ms. Carla opened her door to me. She had a little daughter, and she had a nice house. She would let me eat and cook anything I wanted at her house. She was with an older guy, but he was around her age. His brother began to push up on me and took advantage of me also. But as time went on, Carla would always tell me not to settle for less and to stop letting my baby's daddy and his family dog me out. She would always give me uplifting words. Eventually, she moved out of the projects, and we lost contact. Several years down the line, she got saved and that was a blessing.

During that time, I would go back and forth between my friend's units and stay with different ones.

Renee was my girl. She is no longer here with us. She was killed as a young woman. She put me up on a lot of street game, on how to get my money, and how to not go for the oki doki.

I would like to say thanks to Tina for opening her house up to me. She always made a way of escape for me, and she taught me a little something-something about how to survive in the streets.

As I got a lot older and began to work, I would drink and didn't have anywhere really to go. My girl Sam opened her door for me. There were times where I knew I was so drunk that if I had driven, I probably would be dead or have killed someone else. Thanks a lot for keeping it real and letting me sleep in your daughter's room. Good looking out. We did a lot of crazy partying, but the good part about you was when the party was over, you allowed me to come in your house and lay my head down. You always said to this day can't nobody do your hair like me. Your sister and I weren't as close, but we had our own little relationship. It wasn't too many people in the project that she messed with, but I was one. Thanks for your support.

Little Miss Blondie loved her some me. She always had my back in the salon from sun up to sun down. She worked it out. At the end of the day, if I didn't meet my quota, she would still turn right around and pay. I appreciate her- much love. She never ever got in between her sister and me when her sister was tripping. If anything, she would get on my side and check her sister when it came to me. I still have much love for my cousin. Anyone else that I missed, don't take it personally.

I would like to give a special shout out of blessings over the whole fifty gangs, and since I was married in the seventies and eighties, I release a special covering of God's healing, deliverance and protection around them. No color lines. I release a blanket of peace, healing and deliverance over South Central LA and the surrounding areas. I come against the spirit of tribe and witchcraft and every controlled substance, in Jesus' name.

Chapter Four

My Rose of Sharon

Evalina Dent

MY ROSE, you are the most valuable flower in the garden. Without you, a garden loses its value; it depreciates. You are beautiful when you are small and closed in, but as you grow and sprout out, you are even more beautiful. There are certain extraordinary qualities that you have that must go nationwide. But, you must first be pruned, cultivated and handled with care. You have a heart that's as sweet as the flower smell, but when handled incorrectly, your thorns will prick and most of the times draw blood. The thorns are also a don't-come-to-close mechanism. If people make it pass the thorns, they will see your true beauty. You have seen a lot, been through a lot, and have done a lot. But for such a time as this, God wants you to know His blood is the greatest blood that has ever existed and that will ever exist. It's time to denounce Satan's blood and pronounce Jesus' blood. You are a great asset to the kingdom of heaven. I see a multitude of all different types and colors of roses, a vineyard of them. God said the harvest is plentiful, but the labors are few. Allow God to use you to turn that few into a crew. Always remember, God has given you beauty for ashes. Mommy loves you.

With my first born, I had no idea what I was in for, and to this day, she stills give me a run for my fun.

When she was about nine years old, she was cooking full-course meals and babysitting her two sisters. On the weekends, she would come to the salon and assist me by shampooing and blow-drying my clients' hair. Most of my clients were friends and family. By the time she hit thirteen, she felt like a little grown woman, and she was a big girl. When Nesha was about thirteen years old, I told her that she couldn't go to the projects any more. She wanted to go anyway. I guess she had her little eyes wide open and didn't want to listen to me because she had such adult responsibilities at such a young age.

One day, I told her not to go out. She said that she would hurt herself and that she was going anyway. So, I fixed her. At least, I thought I did. I called her grandmother, and she told me to call the people. I said, "Oh no. I'm not going down that road again. You are not fixing to get me caught up again." She laughed and said, "No. I'm talking about the big men with the strait jackets. They will handle her and scare her straight, and you will have no more problems with her." I called, and she must have heard them and seen them at the door. She ran out the sliding door with no shoes on and called one of her project friends. She came for her, and when I caught up with her, I began to compromise with her a lot because I did not want to lose her completely to the projects.

I had never been a mother before. She was my guinea pig. The more children I had, the more I learned. My last two really catch it because the Holy Ghost is really leading and guiding me with them. They don't like it one bit.

As time went on, Nesha grew more and more disrespectful, but I couldn't let one bad apple spoil the whole bunch. It can be contagious with most kids. What they see one child get away with, they try it. My daughter next to her didn't try it, but the next one did, and I had to nearly put a hole in her tail.

I started learning real fast from my first mistakes. The bible says to beat them. It won't kill them. If you don't get them, they will get you. Or, when they are older, the police will get them. I believe when the government told the parents to stop whipping their children, and when they took the swats and prayer out of school, the death rate and prison toll rose. It is sad to say, and by the way, everybody wants to stereotype our culture and talk about it. But a lot of people have the power and the resources to help; however, they don't. They take on a crab mentality and keep it pushing as far away from the problem as they can. They are so brained washed that they think they are not even from the same culture.

At one time or another, I can say that a lot of our black men didn't want to work; a lot of their jobs were committing 187's and selling drugs. I am sad to say they were very successful at it and were content right in the hood, but there were so many. Today, they are tired of that lifestyle and want something different, but that's all they know. I believe that they are entrepreneurs; they are survivors. They can take a little bit of nothing and turn it into something big.

What I'm trying to say is they need help. They need resources. For those that have felonies and even those that don't, they feel trapped. What does a person do when backed up into a corner? They come out fighting. They need training schools that will guarantee jobs. Let's help to get them off the streets, not by putting them in jail or six feet under, but by placing them in schools, on jobs, in their own homes. Let's help the girls in the hood become young ladies and proud mothers and the hommies become young men, real men, working men, businessmen, proud fathers and sons. I am one that made it out of the hood, and one of my goals is to open businesses that will help them with jobs.

Let's get back to Nesha. As my daughter got older, I had to leave her with her aunty. She would help her cook and sell dinners and whatever else she was selling. It hurt me to my heart to leave my baby in the projects, but as I look back I can say if it was good for the goose, it was good for the gander. I gave my parents a hard time. I am so sorry for what I did to my parents to this day, but I believe it must have been a part of the plan. It seemed as though history was repeating itself.

A couple of years later in 1997, I needed some money. My friend Sherita told me she had a hook up- a way to go and get some money. So, I rolled out with her. As soon as we got out to the city we were going to, we had to stop and get some gas. The police pulled up behind us and began to harass us. They searched the car and asked me for my name. They didn't need to know my name; I wasn't the driver, but I told them my name. They had already told her that she was under arrest and asked me to step out of the car because I was under arrest for possession of sales. I said, "Not me. There must be a mistake." They were so rude to me. They treated me like a common criminal. Those days were over for me. They took us to jail.

It had to be a Friday because we had to stay in there for the weekend at least or get bailed out. My dad said, "Go on and stay in there for the weekend. You can handle it. Stick it out." I said, "Okay." It was devastating, and it was right before New Year's. Yes, I spent New Year's in jail away from my kids. What a bummer! Previously, I had a couple of driving warrants, but I had gone to court, and they had been handled. Therefore, I should not have been arrested that night.

They had to move me from one city to the next one, and it took a long time. It seemed like forever. When I got to the twin towers, they had all kind of stuff going on. I was so timid. I was just minding my own business, and I didn't have any money so the gay girls were giving me stuff. I was eating it, but it wasn't going down.

One day, I went to use the phone, and I was talking to my dad. He was saying, "You only have a day or so for your court date." I started boo whooing and crying. One of the ladies came and touched me a certain way, and I must have turned into a different person on her. They thought I was going fifty one fifty (crazy), but when I finally went to court, the judge apologized and released me. He said I had already completed my probation.

I had not gotten into any more trouble since my first arrest, so they let me go home. Sherita told me this year that she had the money all along but just wanted to go another route. We both learned something from that. I learned not to be so quick to leave my kids because if I can't take them with me I shouldn't go because there is a possibility I won't even make it back to them. So, if you're going somewhere to do something that you can't do with your kids, don't even do it.

I met a young girl one day, and she brought her baby over to my niece to babysit, so she could go and fight. I told my niece not to watch the baby. I got up and went to the porch and stopped the girl. I told her, "Anywhere you can't take your baby you don't need to go. Never go looking for trouble. If it comes to you, try to get out of it. If you cannot, then handle it, but don't let nobody pump you up to go to a fight and leave your baby because there is a chance that you won't make it back to him." She went on anyway.

Several years later, I heard that she never did make it back to her baby. She went to the fight, and someone was killed in a freak accident. She has been in jail for it ever since. May God have mercy on her, her family, and all of those involved. You see, I spent more time in jail for something that I had already paid for when I had first got arrested fifteen years ago. I couldn't do the time then either. I know the saying, 'If you can't do the time, don't do the crime.'

When I was arrested in 1986, I cried like a baby for my dad to get me out. He did just that with the help of a very good friend Mr. Up. He was always good to me. I used to be one of his young tenders, but he was a little too possessive for me. When I called him, he put up money and his mama's house to bail me out. Good looking out. Even the times when I needed to get a place for me and my kids, he had my back even though I had to give him a little something something. But it cost me more than I bargained for.

When I got out of jail, I received a call. Ms. C told me that my daughter was in the hospital in surgery, and my heart was racing. When I arrived, I saw her grandmother, and she said that my daughter was having a miscarriage. She was about fifteen years old, and I thought she was still a virgin. I took her home. I didn't beat her because she bled so much. I thank God she's alive. She came and moved back home and went to school where we lived, but she still would make her way back to those projects.

I remember one late night; she was hanging out there about a year later. She was waiting for one of my friends to bring her home, and she wound up falling asleep in the car in the back seat. She was a heavy sleeper, but on top of that she would struggle with being attacked by the enemy in her sleep where he would try and smother her. She would try to wake up, but she couldn't. She would always tell me that at home she would hear us and everything around her, but she just couldn't wake up.

This particular night, the same thing happened. She said she heard when they got in the car and when one of the girls began to drive. Another girl was in the front seat. They drove out of the garage and approached Gage and Hooper Ave. Some Mexicans started to follow their car. The Mexicans were already in a shootout with another car. Then, they started shooting at the girls, as if the girls were a part of the shootout. Nesha heard everything that was going on, but she couldn't move. The passenger kept calling her name. The last time she called her name, she lifted her head which was lying on her arm. A bullet went through her arm, but she never got all the way up. She acted like she was dead or asleep. She didn't even tell the other girls in the car that she had been shot.

My friend was driving the car backwards to where she started to drive it. The Mexicans were still shooting at them. Then, they hit a fire hydrant, and the guys got out of the car to finish them off. They thought they were some other guys, and the driver was screaming saying, "We're girls. Please don't shoot." They thought our friend in the passenger seat was a boy because she had short hair. When they saw that she was a girl, they left and then the girls called me.

I took Nesha to the hospital, and I went to see the car the next day. There was a big hole right where my daughter's head was lying. I bet the devil was trying to set her up for that way back when she was a little girl, but God is faithful. He spared her life. Thank you, my Lord. I have so much to thank you for.

When I took her back for her checkup, right when she was about to get released, her nurse asked me spontaneously if I wanted her to have a pregnancy test. I said yes. We were about to leave, and he said let me check the results. "Oh yes; it's positive." I said, "What?" I did not expect that at all, but the timing was something else because I felt like I could have lost my child, but then I was gaining a grandchild. I was hurt and upset, but I was so grateful for life. I didn't have any room for any negativity about a new life. There was no doubt about it; he was coming forth.

She had a pretty good and healthy pregnancy, and the closer to her delivery time, the more excited I got. The young man she had the baby for was my boy. He was like a son even though his mom and I were rivals. Our crews stayed into it. I had to handle her too in my old days, but she's cool now. I have no problems with her other than her not doing her part with our grandson like I feel like she should. My grandson feels the same, and you can quote me on that. Anyway, her son used to be on our side of the tracks and stayed with us most of the time.

Before my daughter got pregnant, I remember one day telling her and him not to go there sexually because I really liked him as a son, and if he went there, that would turn him into my enemy. Yea, I understood when Jesus said if you're not with me, you're against me. So, if you messed with my daughter, you messed with me. I was trying my best to keep her on lock. I used to do pretty outrageous things.

For example, one night my daughter was going with this other young boy, and they were at a party on Central and Fifty-Seventh. I walked into the party, stopped him from dancing, snatched her out and told him, "Don't lie to me. I know you took my daughter's virginity. Don't try to lie. I told you from the get go, if you feel you wanted to do it, to go do it with someone else, not that one."

I was standing in the middle of them, and my daughter was behind me. He was saying, "I didn't do nothing." He was looking at me like I was crazy, but later on I found out that my daughter was behind me pleading with him not to say anything. But I was convinced that she had had sex, so I went to him. But she had backtracked and went with

Lil' Man, and her boyfriend really was a friend and had her back. He didn't say anything even though I found out that she crossed him. He was on her, and she gave it to her ex. She said to me later, "Mama, I did lose my virginity that night. I don't know how you knew but you knew. You just didn't know with who." Yea, she fooled me on that one because I knew she wasn't a tramp. I knew her to be a one-boy girl. She got it from her mama. I did the best I could. I did not believe in having sex with more than one guy at a time- literally.

One day, I must have been looking for her and couldn't find her. I went over to her friend G's house. That was my boy and still is to this day. But when it came to my first born, I just didn't play. I went over there and knocked their door down. They did not open it quickly enough. All I was thinking about was someone was on top of my baby. It turned out that she was not in there. When her homeboys told her about it, they said, "Your mama crazy. We didn't know who she was." They were into it with some people, and they were on the other side of the door with a big gun. I will say the love and determination of a mother, and my father too, because he never cared about the projects or nobody in it. Leave it up to him and he would have been blown them up.

So, she gave it up. So, my baby was having a baby, and she started spending more and more time with him and his family. But, she still went to school and worked with me part time because she loved money. Yea, I know. The bible says 'for the love of money is the root of evil.' I would always tell her that she got it from her grandmother.

For all who knew my mom, you know it's not her because she gives out all of hers.

When she was about six or seven months, I spontaneously popped up over to her boyfriend's house, where she was practically staying. I walked up the stairs and walked in his room and told his brother, "I needed some privacy." He walked out, and Nesha followed him. He was looking like please don't leave me, please don't. I began to talk to him and told him the baby would be there in less than two months and I hadn't seen anything he bought him. I had been doing all the spending but I knew he was a good little baby daddy from seeing how he took care of his daughter before my grandson.

I told him to pack a bag, and I kidnapped him. I took him home with us on our territory, and his mom or nobody had nothing to say. I know his brother wanted to say something, but he couldn't fade me, so he didn't try. So he came on with no problem and was very respectful. We cooked, played around, talked, and went to go swimming, but the pool was closed due to something foul swimming in the pool. Use your imagination there please.

The day before he left, I asked him his intentions with my daughter about marriage and everything. He looked at her and said, "Evelyn, you wouldn't marry me would you?" She said, "No," and giggled, which meant she really wanted to. One thing she can't say is she has never been proposed to. So, we had a shotgun wedding, and they jumped the broom.

A couple of months went by, and my daughter and he would have their little differences. I would hear little stuff about him dissing her, but she was a sprung dumb nut. I wasn't. He was my boy, but I wasn't for no mess. The only time I can say he disrespected me was at one of my family's parties. I walked up and checkmated the situation. He started to talk but was walking at the same time in the opposite direction than I was, so I still don't count that against him because he had enough respect for me to not allow me to hear a word that he was saying.

The time for the baby shower came, and it had to be scheduled on her birthday. She didn't like it one bit, but I had already told her having a baby was going to take a lot from her. But, she was in such denial. Let her tell it, to this day, I'm in denial because she is still a hot spoiled mess. Nobody did it but me, and she's almost thirty.

At her baby shower, she was pouting and would not come out to the baby shower. We had it in a large gym. It was decorated beautifully, and there were plenty of food and gifts. She said she wanted to know where her gifts for her birthday were. When she saw me spend all that money on the baby shower, she was sick. Different people were giving her money, like my aunties, and she got money from her boyfriend. She saw that the baby had more than enough to where she locked up on his. Oh, but she paid it back with great interest because the sky is the limit with how much she buys him.

It was getting close for the baby to come. It was the end of the year and of the 1900s. She was nine months, so we were going for, yes, a new millennium baby. The State of California was offering one million dollars for the first baby born on January 1, 2000. We had to move out of our place and didn't have anywhere to go, at least nowhere that my kids didn't mind staying. I had to go down a list, and the only place that they agreed to go to was my legal's (my sister-in-law) house. She welcomed us with open arms.

One night when we were coming in, my kids went straight to the back house. I had another sister-in-law that lived in the front house, and she had company, one of which was a cousin-in-law that just could not stand me. She was my young homegirl who had no respect and went for bad. I was saved at that point, but she would say all kinds of stuff to me, call me all kinds of names, and say what she would do. I didn't say or do anything. That was some of the stuff I had to go through as I was coming out of the world. I held my peace.

That particular night, she started in on me and was talking about my kids, saying I was homeless and I wasn't nothing. She said she wanted a fade, and I walked outside to go to the back. She was talking so loud to where everybody including my kids came outside. She was going on and on to where before I knew it my first born politely walked around the car and the bushes. The girl was still talking, and out of nowhere, my daughter took off on her. They started fighting, and all I could see at a point was the girl's leg lifting up to kick my daughter in her stomach. So, I grabbed her away from my daughter.

I was forced to fight- the love of a mother and the soon-to-be grandmother. I told her, "You want to fight? Let's go." I hadn't fought in so long. I thought I had forgotten how to fight. One of my little daughters hit her too. We fought for a minute or two, and I won. Let my kids tell it, I was moving in slow motion. I thought I was getting down, and the Lord knows I was so tired and out of breath. I was like please somebody break it up; when is somebody going to it break it up? She probably could have got me but for one, she was drunk and I was sober, and for two, she was about seven to ten years under me. She could have out-winded me, not to mention I was struggling with asthma. Thank God somebody broke it up, but that's my girl now. She said my kids and I double-teamed her. I'll let you be the judge of that.

That was Christmas Eve, and once we made it to sleep, Nesha said it was time to have the baby. So, he was not a new millennium baby. But guess what? Yes, we had a Christmas baby. That's even better to be born on the day that we celebrate our Savior's birthday. She had him at Martin Luther King Hospital, and I just knew that she was going to be in so much pain to where she wouldn't think about having another one for a mighty long time.

That was her doctor's first delivery. Now we know, the doctor had let the epidural stay in Nesha's back until she almost had the baby. Nesha and the baby were out of it. When she went to sleep, she was about three centimeters, and when she woke up she was ten. It was time to go.

When she was about six months, I had told her that I had a dream that she had the baby, and it was a boy. He came out half way. He was cute, and he went back in. When they were rolling her down the hall to the delivery room, he came out and she said, "It's coming out." She felt his head come out. I guess he said, "Let me take a sneak peek," and then said, "Naw. I'm out of here. I'm going back in." Like Nicodemus said, "What must I do to be saved?" Jesus said, "You must be born again." Then Nicodemus said, "How shall I go back into my mother's womb?" Jesus said, "No, born again in the spirit." My grandson will be able to say he was born three times, three births (two in the natural and one spiritual).

Chapter Five

My Lily of the Valley

Temila Dent

MY LILY OF THE VALLEY, you were created to last from the very beginning, but you really didn't have a chance. You went through the roughest and toughest storms, but you held on. You are one of God's favored flowers. You have survived in the greatest heat. The more heat, the greater the shine. You grow under the greatest pressure. The more the pressure, the greater the anointing. You are the most beautiful and purest of them all. You have endured all types of hurt and pain physically, emotionally and spiritually, but you're still here. What the devil meant for bad and tried to use to take you out, God is using to cause you to sprout and bring you out. You will go many places and do many things to decree and declare Jesus' name. My lily, you are so very special to me but much more precious and special to our daddy. So, be exactly who he created you to be. Remember these scripture: "For greater is he that's in me than he that is in this world" and "I can do all things through Christ who strengtheneth me." Love, Mommy.

I met boyfriend number three one day when I was walking across the tracks in the projects with one of my friends. He was with a mutual friend Ronald, and he asked him my name and who I was. Ronald told him my name, but he also told him that I was Stumper's girl. But after going through so much with Papa, I was pretty fed up. Mr. Al asked me what was up with me and if I had any room for him in my life. I blushed and said, "Maybe so." He asked me for my number, and I gave him the number where I lived. I was still living with Papa, his mom and his siblings, but I did ask Ms. C if I could give him the number. She said, "Yes." She didn't like the way Papa treated me.

So, Mr. Al and I started going out, but I was still living with Papa and sleeping with him, but I started not liking him. For one, Papa was going out with Mr. Al's sister, and she was cool. I went to elementary with her, and we even talked about her going out with my baby's daddy. I told her, "It's cool. You got my baby's daddy, and I got your brother." I really started to dig him. We would go out of the projects to his family's house on the west side, and we would go to night clubs, out to eat, or we would just stay up all night doing grown stuff. He was something else. He was much more mature and experienced than I was, but I liked him. I liked the way he did things. He always dressed nice and was well groomed at all times. That was my kind of man, not to mention how nice he smelled. He was a real turn on.

As time went on, Papa started to show his jealousy even though he had plenty of girls. I remember one day Mr. Al and I had went to the hair salon to get our hair done. Back then, we had Jeri Curls. So, on that particular day, our hair was locked up, and we were dressed alike by accident. We had on white pants and grey Members Only jackets and some fresh white K-Swiss. Mr. Al walked me home, and he left to go wherever he was going. As I turned the corner of Papa's house, he came and called me a bad name and pushed me down in the mud and tried to hit me with the top of a trash can. How humiliating that was, but he knew it was over for him. I didn't want him at all. Even though I was living with him, I had been stopped having intercourse with him. It was on with me and Mr. Al. We were so close that he had taken me to meet his mom. She would share her food recipes with me.

Let me tell you, his mom and his older sister could cook. So, we were going out for about six months, and I found out that I was pregnant. I was more months than I thought I was. Remember, I was still having relations with my old boyfriend because of my living situation. So, one day Mr. Al's little sister came up to me and asked me if I was carrying her brother's baby, and I couldn't answer her because at the time I really didn't know. All I had to do was go to the doctor and find out how many months. Before she walked away, she said, "My mom is excited, and she wants to know if it is her grandbaby."

I went to the doctor, and I found out that the baby was not his. I was already pregnant when we got together, or I got pregnant in the first couple of months of our relationship. I let him and his family know that the baby wasn't theirs. They were all disappointed. At that point, my relationship with Mr. Al didn't grow stronger.

So, my sister came to get me from the projects and moved me to Pomona with her to her first apartment. Now we're talking a long distant relationship. We didn't have a phone, but I was in love with that dude. I was so crazy about him that I would walk all the way to the phone booth to call him every day at the same time. But one day, he dumped me over the phone at the phone booth. He told me, "This long distant relationship isn't working for me, and by the way I've been talking to another girl. She's much older and mature, so I'm going to be with her. It's over." My heart dropped to the floor of the phone booth. To top it off, it was raining. That was a cold rainy walk home, but I dealt with it and accepted it. But, I didn't like it one bit.

Eventually, I left Pomona and his relationship didn't last too long with the other girl. We started going out again, but it was a lot different. I remember on one night, I went with him to over to a guy's house that he used to work for. He was a friend of his as well. We were there by ourselves at first, and then the guy came in. At that time, I believe we were upstairs in one of the rooms. The house was big and scary. Mr. Al was saying that he was over there to come up on some money and stuff and that the guy liked young girls. He said I didn't have to do anything with him. The guy used to go out and pay so many of my friends, but he was ugly. It was just something about me when it came to a man who was not easy on the eyes. I didn't want nothing to do with him.

Mr. Al came in the room that I was in and told me that the man wanted to mess with me. I said *here I go again* to myself, but I told him he had to be out of his rabbit mind. I told him, "I'm your girl. What's really going on?" He said, "I know, but he been getting high, and he's tripping. He locked all the doors, and he said that's the only way you can get out." I was scared but still bold and courageous. I told him, "No." My heart was pounding. The whole house was dark, and it was about two o'clock in the morning or later. I told Mr. Al to help me get out through the window from upstairs and he did. I said that I will never get in that predicament again.

But as time went on, I continued to go out with him, and it almost happened again. One night, I had gone with him to his family reunion. We went over to his aunty's house on the west side afterwards. We were doing something we had no business doing in the restroom when everybody was asleep. At least, I thought they were. That was until Mr. Mr. Al left out of the restroom and his cousin came in right after him and said, "My turn." I said *oh my God here we go again I know I told myself that I wouldn't get in this predicament again but here I go.* All this is going on in my mind while he was trying to rape me. I told him, "No, you got me twisted. I don't get down like that." He was persistent. At that point, I knew I had to be more aggressive. I stated to speak louder, and I told him that if he didn't leave me alone and get out that I would wake up the whole house. He turned around and left out. I was so embarrassed and humiliated. I told Mr. Al later, and he said he didn't know nothing about it and that his cousin was a pervert like that even when they were younger. He said his cousin tried to mess with his sister, who was his first cousin. After that I never really trusted him anymore, and our relationship began to fade away.

When I found out I was pregnant, I had started using drugs at that time, and I just didn't want to stop. So, I had set in my mind that I was going to abort her. I continued to smoke premos, but I couldn't drink because I would get too sick. I did everything else like fighting, climbing poles, and crazy stuff.

At my sixth month, Papa begged me not to do it. So, I kept her. Yes, I had planned to commit murder on my unborn child at my sixth month. I had her six weeks later; she was only two and a half pounds at birth. I guess she wanted get out before I killed her. She is known as my miracle child. To God be the glory.

Once I had seen that it was too late to abort her, I stopped using drugs and started taking better care of myself. However, she was born without a complete digestive system, and no doctors in the state of California would perform the surgery. A doctor was flown in that re-routed her intestines.

After the surgery, she came home for a while. I had my own duplex house for me and my two girls. The hospital would send the nurse to my home to check to be sure everything was okay. And it was, but I remember telling the nurse that the baby kept boo booing and throwing up. The nurse said to let the doctor know at her next doctor's appointment.

When we saw the doctor, he said that she needed to be hospitalized, but I had no idea what was ahead of me. My life was in for something I could never prepare for. I never thought it would have happened to me, especially at that time when I thought I was doing so well. But I guess the children's hospital thought differently.

When I took her to the hospital, I would go back and forth to see her. I didn't want to trade her for another baby because I loved my baby. I took good care of her, especially for the age that I was. When I went to visit her a couple of days after she was hospitalized, the nurse told me that my baby was in the custody of the Department of the Children's Social Services meaning they had taken her from me. They said that she was suffering from failure to thrive meaning she was starving to death. You tell me what black person is not going to feed her baby. If anything, we over feed them, especially if they are given free milk and food stamps. It was not the EBT back then. I had the book of stamps. EBT is this new world order stuff.

I would catch the bus to see her. Even if it was raining, sleeting or snowing, I was there. They would still let me come and see her, but they said that when she got better, if she got better, that I couldn't take her home with me. So a couple more days went by, and the doctors wanted to talk to me again. It was so scary. Sometimes my dad would come and talk to them, and her grandma on her dad's side would be there as well, but for the most part I was a young teen mom in a real big world having to make real-life decisions over another human being's life.

In that meeting, the doctors told me that the surgery was successful. Normally, the surgery is performed on adults. It had not been performed on a child that small. So, when they stitched her up, they didn't double stitch her. It caused poison, toxins and waste to go into her body and contaminate her system. That's why she couldn't hold anything in. She was actually trying to survive. She would keep emptying out everything.

It seemed like they would have dropped the case against me and given my baby back, but that was too much like right. They were too scared of admitting they were wrong and me suing them. But, I didn't sue them at that point. I was just so grateful that they had saved my baby's life. I couldn't see myself suing the doctors that saved her life, but I know differently now. That was malpractice and wrongful accusations. But, my baby was fine.

I had to go through the court system to get her back and then her money-hungry grandma that I let keep her so that she didn't have to be with strangers tried to not just keep her but wanted to take my other daughter too. But my older daughter wanted to be with her mama, but they tried to bribe her with money and gifts. Her grandma called her into a little room before we went into court and told her to lie on me. My daughters' aunt spoke up and told Nesha to tell the truth. She did, and the court released Mila to me. But, she had to spend her first birthday and Christmas with a Caucasian family. She has been through a lot in her life as well because she had been dealing with the spirit of rejection since she first got in my womb.

She is my most special child; we have a bond that no one can come between. We have had our good and bad times, but mostly good. She is someone that has always had my back, even when she didn't want to. I love her for real. We call each other BFFL (best friend for life), and not many mothers and daughters can say that. I remember when she called herself having a boyfriend, and she went and did the do. Now, I have whooped my other kids but never Mila. But when she did that and came in the house late, I slapped her up a couple of times. She was devastated, and she was eighteen.

I have always been overprotective of her. I don't like her to be too far from me to this day. Most of the time, I know she likes the attention, but sometimes she's like give me a break lady. [I'm laughing.]

She has now given me five beautiful grandchildren, but the doctors told me that she would never be able to live a normal life and that her life expectancy would be around thirteen to eighteen, if that. What the devil meant for bad, God turned it for our good. Thank you my Lord, for your grace and your mercy. It's been more than enough. Even though she has kids of her own, her house, and her own money, we all know age don't make you grown. But it's having your own and being independent. But I still had the spirit of control. It took a while for me to come to that realization, but I saw that I was under the influence of a controlling spirit when I would try to keep a count on her money and her honey.

Here are some words I spoke when took a moment to vent and get free:

I am in a place of expectancy; it seems so dark, dry, lonely and empty. I know that I'm yet full and about to burst and give birth to greatness, as I sit with great anticipation and full of despair. I know that it is not in the feelings or emotions. But one thing I do know is my destiny must and shall prevail. Every evil, vindictive thought, scheme and words that were spoken over my life will not prosper. Every itchy ear will not be fed or glorified. You shall hear my triumph. You shall hear my testimonies, my victories, and my prosperities. You shall hear my anointing whether you like it or not. It's mine; God gave it to me. I had to endure much to get it, and you can't have it. As a matter of fact, you can't even handle it. You can't fit it; it was tailored made just for me. So, do yourself and me a favor: get over it. It's time to get over it and get your own. Get your eyes, hearts and minds out of other folk's stuff. God will allow you to go through some stuff to become an over comer.

So, you feel like you can suffer and be persecuted for God's name sake. But you haven't really even been through it. Look what Christ had to endure. It's time to go through our trials and tribulations. Can you pass an emergency broadcast test? Will you stay faithful and tuned into God for further directions or will you panic and tune into the worldly system or another name you might be familiar with? That's called compromising. You find yourself moving back and forth. One minute you love God. He's your boo, your everything: Jehovah Jira, your provider, your Alpha and Omega.

You begin ponder in your mind and to check some of your old avenues, some of the old ways you used to handle things. Yeah, I know because I did it. I was in bondage on Section Eight for over five years when I only needed it for two or three years. The rest of the years, I was living a lie. I was in captivity in my own home. I had to prepare and figure out the best way that I was going to tell my annual lie. That was when I had to go to my yearly interview. My income was getting too high. It had me in poverty mentality, focusing on staying low enough to meet their guidelines, not to mention they wanted to run and rule my home.

I remember when one of my girls had graduated from high school, and she decided to move out of state to go to college. I had to report by letter that she moved, but she didn't stay out there any longer than a year. So, when she came home, I thought I was doing the right thing by writing them a letter to let them know that my daughter was back home. They had the audacity to politely send me a letter stating that they would not be able to allow her to move back into my home at that point. I wondered *what kind of mess is this?*

What mother can tell her nineteen-year-old daughter that she can't move back home because she is being controlled by the government and is afraid to trust God all the way and step out on faith and move forward? I wasn't going to be able to tell my baby she couldn't come home. When she did come home, I was really feeling like a prisoner in my own house.

A lot of these assistance programs that help you are just a set up to keep you in a poverty state of mind being completely dependent and controlled by the government. My opinion is if you really need it, it is as a stepping stone. It's easy to get on and get a job and move on, but the transition is not that easy for most people. You must report your income, or they will throw you off the program. A lot of people can't afford to pay rent plus eat. There isn't anything for the in-between; either you're rich or poor. Looking back, I remember when I used to buy EBT from other people. Yes, food stamps, for those of you who don't know what EBT is.

I got convicted in Christ for doing that, thank God. I'm not talking about nobody else. It was about me getting free. It's about the man in the mirror. I just needed to be real and obedient. When I first got convicted from buying food stamps, I began to think more about the kids who were going without. The government is very intelligent, and they will not give each family more than needed to make it through the next month. My second conviction in Christ was when I began to think about the laws of the land. Do you think I would have been in jeopardy of going to jail for breaking the law? The reason I'm sharing this situation with you is because two of the enemy's greatest weapons are deceit and deception. Don't get caught with your pants down or your hand in the cookie jar.

My third conviction in Christ was when I was on SSI. I was on when I first had a nervous breakdown. God healed me. He restored my mind, my body, and my spirit. But, I continued to get the check even though I knew it was wrong. I wasn't walking in my complete healing. I was tying God's hands every time I cashed the check because He wanted to give me so much more. But it was according to my faith.

As time went on, I began to feel worse and worse. I would tell myself that I was going to stop the check that month, but there would always be a reason or something that came up that would cause me not to give it up. I would say I'm not doing all that good. I can wait. I would be in torment month after month, year after year. Something had to give. I had no peace, so I made up my mind and decided that I would no longer be a thief. Then, I denounced the spirits that were attached to me. I gave up SSI. I refused to allow $900 to stop me from receiving nine million. The truth shall always prevail.

As time went on, I began to really struggle. It was bad when I let the check go, but I would not allow the cares of this life to choke me out. I continued to trust and have faith in God. The bible says without faith, it's impossible to please God. That's what I live to do: please Him. So, I stepped out on faith and severed all ties with Social Security. I applied for social security with Jesus Christ, relying and depending on Him with all my heart, mind and soul. God is my resource. He said He will supply all my needs according to His riches and glory.

Maybe you fall short in these areas. Can you really work or do you have a skill, a dream, a vision, or witty idea that you're just sitting down on? Have you allowed God to order your steps or have you been lying to everyone else to where you're beginning to believe your own lies? Go deep and grab the real. Allow God to be glorified. God is glorified when you cut out the things from the world and trust and depend on Him. I had to trust Him with my little, and He turned it into much.

There is something about when you give, especially your tithes and offerings. When you give sacrifices and obedience from your heart it attracts God's attention. He will take action and move on your behave. That's how God is glorified. No one can do it but Him. I was worth a lot of more money than what I was getting. I am also a hair stylist but it was like putting my money in a paper bag with a hole in it. But, I had God's hands tied in another area.

Fourth conviction: as time went on, I was working and making good money. But it seemed like the more I made, the more was spent. It was time for another annual verification. It was time to let it go. Yes, section eight had to go. Section Eight was only paying a small portion of my rent in my large five-bedroom home. So, Section Eight and the house had to go. Yes, I gave up my Section Eight, and I repented to my Father. It is the truth that will make us free.

This system was designed to keep us in bondage. There was something that was tugging and pulling on me to do right, to do good and not evil, to practice what I preach. My spirit was getting more and more hungry for God. When you are not being honest, righteous and holy, the door will open for finances to be cursed. I had to let it go, and when I did, I was so free and free indeed.

The bible said Jesus came to set the captives free and whosoever is free is free indeed. I haven't been homeless or hungry or begged for bread. The word of God says, "I've never seen the righteous forsaken nor his seed begging for bread." SSI and Section Eight had become strongholds in my life. I just couldn't seem to let them go. It even began to contaminate my seeds, so I took control and authority over the spirit of lack, greed, lying, stealing, and every unclean sprit that was attached to me and all my descendants. I denounced and pulled them up and cast them to the pits of hell and sealed them there with the blood of Jesus.

This world system is designed to have you in its complete control. Can you imagine if they took your income, snatched your housing assistance, and told you that they will no longer be able to give you food stamps for you and your family? What will you do to feed you and yours? What price will you pay? Will you do whatever they say? There will come a time when this world will be set in a certain order. Will you be prepared?

Chapter Six

My Wild Flower:
Destined for Destiny

Latrina Jackson

MY WILD FLOWER, you are full of life. You are exactly who God created you to be. When everyone else said no, God said, "It is so." You have been through a lot of hurt and pain, but for such a time as this, you shall come forth from pain to purpose - God's purpose. You were often rejected and seldom accepted. You will always be my baby. There's a bond between you and me, and it's that bond that will help take you to your destiny. You bring beauty to the worst atmosphere. Have no fear; the wild flower is here. You shall come forth like a mighty rushing wind. You can grow in any type of environment, from the most prestigious places to the driest and desolate places. You will survive. Not only will you survive, you will be used to bring life wherever you are. You are not afraid of change. At any given time, you can appear in an unfamiliar land or territory and adapt and flourish. You're not only a wild flower, but you can be transformed into a wild fire for God. Everywhere you go, God will use you to catch everyone you come in contact with on fire for Him, in Jesus' name. I decree it and declare it. It shall come to pass. Always remember, all things work together for the good to those that love God and are called according to His purpose. You were marvelously and wonderfully made, and you are so very beautiful to me. I thank God for allowing me to give birth to someone so great and so beautiful. Love you always, Mommy.

With my wild flower, it was pretty rough from the very beginning. I did something that they say never works out right: I got into a relationship with my one of my best friends. At least, I thought he was. But, he turned out not to be after all.

My wildflower has come a mighty long way. She has come from a place where she never trusted anyone. She always thought someone was putting her down or was talking about her or didn't care for her. She was the most negative person that I had ever met in my life with no exaggeration at all. I could not believe that I could have anyone with such negativity and low self esteem. When I look back over my life, when I was her age and maybe a little younger, I made a lot of stupid decisions too. The things she accepted from different guys were unreal. I would get so upset to where I didn't even want to deal with her at times, but I had to stop and look back and think about the things that I had done with different relationships. That's what made me have more compassion for her.

As a little girl, Latrina struggled with the spirit of rejection, and it came through her father. Let me tell you the story of her conception. By this time, I was on boyfriend number three. He was dark and handsome to me, and a lot of other chicks thought the same, as I found out later in the game. I met him when my girls and I would go down to his neighborhood to see him and his friends. They were from the bottoms, in the forties, and we were from the fifties. But, we didn't let turfs or neighborhoods stop us back then. We went wherever we wanted to go. We would hang out, drink, smoke weed, and crack jokes on each other. There were two of his boys that were so funny. They say one of them actually turned out to have had some funny business going on later down the line, but I don't know for sure. It's not my business, so I really shouldn't be speaking on it. That's why I'm not going to say his name or even get close to his name.

I remember going down to that neighborhood a couple of years before with my big sister; she used to go with a guy who lived there. He was her second love, and he had a brother who liked me. It didn't go anywhere at all. As time went on, I started going down there on my own. We would pick and choose whom we would go out with from each crew. I know if the girls discussed it, the guys did too. But for the most part, the guys did the choosing. If the girl liked him, they went for it. But if she didn't, it faded away. My cousin and I really hit it off with two of the guys and had long-term relationships. Mine was with Casanova.

Casanova started off strong and sweet. At the same time, he was good to me and my kids. He saw that I was a young girl with two kids, and whatever I needed him to do, he did it, including taking me to the hospital to see my baby girl Mila. There were times when we went in to see her, and we would have to wear a mask. But, I didn't like to make my baby feel like she was poison or contagious. So, I wouldn't wear the mask. But, the other people that would take me to see her insisted on wearing it. I really knew he cared for me and mine. When he saw I didn't wear a mask, he didn't wear one either. That drew me closer to him.

He made it a part of his daily routine to take me to see my baby. When I was busy doing other stuff, He would remind me that it was time, and I needed to go to the hospital and visit my baby. That was a blessing. We would go out, hang out, and ride up and down the streets. He wanted to have plenty of you know what. I really didn't like that part about him. Most of the time, even back then, he seemed so nasty. I know the word is perverted. I guess I was having mixed emotions from everything that had happened to me sexually up to that point.

Another time in the beginning of our relationship, one of my uncles that was on drugs had my little sister to go through my window and open my door for him, so he could go in and steal all of my stuff, meaning my money and drugs. Yes, that's the life that I lived. When my uncle stole everything I had, I was devastated. All I could do was cry because that was my rent money, and I had just moved into my first duplex. When Casanova found out, he gave me eight hundred dollars and put me back in the game. So between his money and his honey, I fell head over hills for him. Back in the day, they would call it sprung and dumb. He was insecure and very abusive also. My life with him is a whole other book.

He was so jealous whenever I was around certain people. I knew trust was a fight. Just let me share a little of my life with him. You know, I was still in the game. I was seventeen, and I had my own place because I had to get my life in order so I could have a place for my baby to come home to. A man rented me a really nice duplex. I had the place furnished and everything. I was so excited. I really didn't know what to do, but I winged it through.

He would come over and hang out, and we would do the do like there was no tomorrow. I was so connected to him, but back then we called it sprung. One thing I can say is he wasn't selfish at all. He helped me, and I helped him. He was the only guy that I went out with that I allowed to do anything for my girls, like buy them clothes, toys or anything else. He wasn't just concerned about me, but he was concerned about my girls too. He didn't just take me out; he would take us all out. Back then, you didn't find too many guys that would take the whole package deal without a hidden agenda, if you know what I mean. He got it, but I had a price to pay physically, emotionally, and mentally.

He was very jealous and possessive. I had to let him know every move I made, and if I didn't that gave him a reason to hit me. It didn't take him no time to begin to fight me. It was my natural instinct to rebel. I rebelled against my dad even though I knew I would have to pay the consequences. I found myself accepting that same abuse from my boyfriend. Once again, he loved me and then he hurt me. I thought that was just the way it was supposed to be, sad to say.

I remember one day, there was a particular person in my house. I wasn't doing anything with him and had no intensions. Casanova came in and saw the person leaving and he said, "You think I'm playing with you." He started doing something on the side of the bed and talking at the same time. Then all of a sudden, he rose up real quick. He pushed me into the corner and put a black 38 to my head. He said, "I will kill you." At that moment, he pulled the trigger. I grabbed his hand with both of my hands and said, "No, Casanova." The gun went off and shot me in my right leg as I pulled it from my head. I saw my life flash right before my eyes. I couldn't believe that happened to me. My leg felt like fire had gone through it, but I really couldn't focus on my leg. I was busy focusing on the fact that he almost killed me. I wouldn't have been here to continue to raise my girls.

I would have flashbacks or just sit or lie down and just meditate on what could have happened. I was and I am still so very grateful for God's hand being behind the force that stopped that bullet from going through my head. Casanova was so shocked and scared; he thought that he had taken all the bullets out when he was leaning on the side of my bed. But if you know anything about guns, most of the time there is one left in the chamber. I could have lost my life and ruined my girls' lives and his life also with foolishness. To all who are in crazy, wild abusive relationships: get out while there is still time. To the abuser: stop. It is not worth it. Don't get caught up in something that will be real hard to get out. Some go to a place where they can't get out. No male or female is worth taking another person's life.

Let me get back to my story. Casanova took me to the hospital, and he begged for forgiveness. He told me that he was so sorry, and that it was an accident. He said he was only trying to scare me, so that I wouldn't cheat or be around other guys. When the doctor and the police officer asked me who did it, I lied and said someone in a drive-by. I know now that the doctor and the police could tell that it was a close range shot. And yes, I stayed with him. I was what you would call sickly sprung. I was sprung, young, and dumb. Don't let it be you; it only gets worse.

Time went on. He didn't hit me for a while, but eventually he started it right back up. I believe he couldn't help himself due to where he came from. I found out later that his mom was a prostitute, and he was a trick or a pimp baby. So, he only did what was in him to do. It was up to me to decide just how long I would be a victim in his mad, crazy life. So, I was still in his crazy life, and we were riding. He started accusing me again, and he took me down a dark street, made me get out, and told me to start walking. Then, he pulled out his gun and said, "Run for your life." I ran. He didn't have to tell me twice because I was still gun shocked. I was so scared. How could he dare do me like that after all he had put me through?

I was running and praying, hoping he didn't shoot me on purpose or accident. I saw a light on, and I ran to the house and banged on the door. I was crying, and I told them, "My boyfriend is chasing me with a gun. Can you please let me in?" They were an old couple. One wanted to let me in, but the other didn't because they know how people can act crazy when you get into their business. But, they let me in. Finally, he left. I made it to safety to my grandma's house, which was right down the street. Later, I found out he went and shot the old people's house up. He didn't hurt them, but he probably made it bad for the next girl that might have needed their help.

Later that night, he hit me so hard and gave me my first black eye. I walked to the corner store in the morning and bought some witch hazel. By the time I made it home and was in my restroom looking in the mirror looking at myself and saying to myself how he had already put permanent knots in my lips to this day and now look at my eye, I look a mess, there he was. He popped up out of nowhere. I couldn't have a moment to cry in peace. He showed no comfort. He said, "What you doing? Give me that." He took the witch hazel and poured it down the sink. Oh yes, he sure did. But, I still stayed with him. That wasn't enough. When my young uncle heard about it, he wanted to get him so bad. I knew Casanova kept a gun, and my uncle just wanted to rough him up. But I felt like it would go further than just a fight because my uncle could have handled it either way, but I handled my own business. I didn't want to put none of my family in my mess because I knew I wasn't going to leave him. If anything would have happened to my family, it would be on me.

I remember being so sprung that one time I couldn't get a ride to his spot, so I caught the bus. He lived in the 40's at that time, and I lived in the 50's. I got off the bus and began to walk to his house. I knocked on the door, but no one answered. Out of nowhere I heard loud music coming from up the street playing *He's Strange but I Like It*. It was his car, and I saw him with another chick on his side. From another corner, another girl drove up. She too was coming for him. I stood on the porch with my mouth wide open. He saw me standing on the porch, and he kept right on driving right past me as if he didn't even see me. He didn't even look my way.

I caught the bus back. I was hurt, crying and embarrassed because my cousin Keisha had caught the bus with me. How humiliated I was. I told her and myself that I was done with him. That was it. By the time I got home on the bus, which took about fifteen to twenty minutes, he had driven his chick on-the-side to the west side, which normally would have taken about at least forty minutes. But by the time I made it home, he was there waiting for more. Then he began to tell me exactly what I wanted to hear; he told me, "It wasn't me!" I knew was a lie. It sounded good to me at the time because I wasn't ready to give him up deep inside. You know the saying 'believe none of what you hear and probably half of what you see.'

He was sick and crazy. He would jump on me and then wanted to have crazy sex with me. I couldn't tell him no, not even when Mother Nature visited me. That had only happened once that I can remember. I was at his house, and he wanted to have sex. I said "No," and he bit my breast so hard until I gave in. How nasty and disgusting. I just laid there feeling so filthy and violated. *I just wasn't meant to be this type of girl. What am I doing here?* I asked myself. So after a few years, I was so tired of being abused and accused of messing around with my best friend Black Boy. It didn't make sense. I don't know how many times I had been jumped on for just being around Black Boy. I had no intension of messing around with him at all. He really had a problem with him, but Black Boy and I went all the way back.

So, I finally went on and I told him that it was over. A short time later, he went to jail. I was sad and lonely. On a rainy night, I went out with my hommies and was getting high and drinking. You know drinking leads to other things. I wound up at my best friend's house. I was on the rebound, and you know what happened. Yes, we did it. What a mess! That's a big no no that you don't do: have sex with a close friend, but I did. It was a mess. He would talk so much about what he could do, but when it came to me it was a boom bam thank you ma'am. As quick as it was, guess what? I got pregnant.

He would always say about his girls: if they ever got pregnant and killed his baby what he would do. He said at least let him know. Well, I didn't. As quick as I got pregnant, I got rid of it. Yes, I repented. I told one of our mutual friends, and as time went on, in about three or four weeks we had sex again. You know what? I got pregnant again. I had to keep the baby. I was not having an abortion that close back to back with my young body. So I kept it. I was always a one-man woman. I didn't cheat. I didn't believe in messing around with two or more guys at the same time. At that time in my life. So, I waited a little while and told him that I was pregnant, but he was with somebody else at the time. We had never been an item. We had just messed around at the time, but he was always on me now that I look back.

I can still remember that night that I told him I was pregnant. I was standing in a dark hallway at my granny's house, and I told him that I was pregnant. I was so shocked and hurt when I heard his response. He said, "What you want me to do? What you telling me for?" I said, "It's yours." He responded, "Since you decided to kill the first one, I'm deciding on this one. If you decide to keep it, it's yours not mine."

He held onto his word for about sixteen years. Our daughter had to live with that ridicule all of her childhood. When she would go to the park, the store, or anywhere in the neighborhood, people would ask her questions because she came out looking exactly like him, and he still didn't claim her. Not only did she have to deal with the shame in the neighborhood, but she had to deal with it at home. My sister had a son by his brother, and they were around the same age. My nephew would go over to his grandmother's, but my wildflower couldn't go. It was like she said because you-know-who lived there, and she didn't want any problems with him. But she had an awesome Uncle Keith Wayne. He took care of her like she was his. He never made her feel like her dad was missing because he truly spoiled her.

When I was seven months pregnant with her, I went to visit my ex in jail. He told me he was sorry for everything and asked if I could forgive him. He said he would never hit me again. I went for it since I had got shot all the way down from not only my homeboy but my best friend. I was feeling real low, lonely and angry.

So when he got out, we hooked up. Soon as he came home, he took me shopping for the baby, took me to my doctor's appointment, and even went with me to have her and has been taking care of her ever since. I believe that her dad was into some dark stuff in his early days. He believed differently than I did concerning God. I raised her up in church, but when she got older, she would ask me weird questions about how I know God is real, why would God kill, and is God and the devil playing a game with us. I would have to answer her the best way I knew how. I know that spirit came from her dad.

You really have to be careful who you have a child with. As she went through her life and experiences with drugs and men, God had to deal with her Himself, and I believe that all things work together for the good to those that love God and are called according to His purpose. I also believe that the Lord was shielding her from the influence of her father. She would have been tainted even more because I can tell the difference from all my kids and her because she came from him. I could see the darkness.

I remember he would be dropping lugs about God, and he opened the Webster dictionary and looked up the word *villain.* That was a set that we were from, but he showed me that it meant evil and reckless.

When Latrina reached eighteen, she thought she was grown and decided to go on her own. I didn't take it too well. I told her that my door is not a revolving door and when she leaves to stay gone and don't come back. But that only lasted for a season. She wound up out in Lancaster with my siblings, and boy oh boy, my brother who had been shot and paralyzed had a great influence on their generation. I feel because he felt like his life was pretty much in ruins, he would sabotage our children's purpose and destiny. When it came to mine, God said not so.

When Latrina moved to Lancaster, I was heartbroken and angry. I was deep in church, but I was in a place where I really didn't know what was going on with my child. I had put her in God's hands and was trying my best not to take her back out of them. As time went on, she had begun to experience hard mind-blowing drugs, such as ecstasy. That is a hallucinogenic drug that was sent to wipe her generation out.

Some of the youngsters would pop those pills and go and do drive-by's. A lot of them would have sexual fantasies and get caught up doing things that they wouldn't have ever done if they weren't on the ecstasy. It is a drug that really does permanent damage to the mind. It was so bad to where I didn't know my own child. I had to pray like never before.

One day, my sister's bishop called me and told me to come and get my daughter because the death spirit was in the area where she was. I said, "I'll try to get there when I can." She called me back and said, "Come now. It is life or death." So, I made up my mind and was released from God to go because my thing was that I didn't want to get in God's way. I got an A+ in that area.

I began to drive, and it started to rain, then pour. I really knew that I had to get there, and I don't know what time I got there, but that bishop was still there. She waited on me and counseled us. God used her to draw Latrina back to God.

She came back home, but it seemed like her mind was blown. She thought everyone was against her. She was living with me, and she met a guy. I told her I didn't know about him. I couldn't put my finger on it. Normally, I know people, but he had his stuff to the tee. He had it on lock. He would be so nice to her, but she would just hit him and talk to him like crap. I told her to stop and explained she would start it, but he would finish it. As time went on, we would run into different people, and they would say how much of a terrible kid he was. He said he had changed, so we gave him the benefit out of the doubt and allowed him to come into our world.

Before we knew it, he was turning our world upside down. He had disrespected me by having the police at my house. He was jumping on her, but I'll say this, I had spoken to a girl that my daughter had gotten into it with. She said, "All stuff to the side. Your daughter don't know what she's getting into." I told Latrina, but she continued anyway. He turned out to be very abusive and very stubborn. When he wants something to go his way, he blocks out everything and everybody. It will take the police to stop him. I'm not saying he's all bad because there is such a good part of him. I guess you can say when he's good, he's good, and when he's bad, he's bad. He has had it pretty bad in his life.

Now, my daughter has two beautiful sons. She recently sent me a text me saying one of her boys is so bad and asking why he has a mind of his own. I told her that I saw those similar familiar spirits in him that I saw in his dad, so we had to pray and cast out all demonic activity and assignments through the blood line up off of him.

As I wrote this section, something came to my remembrance. While she was carrying my grandbaby, her boyfriend spent a lot of time over our house. I would wake up in the morning and pray like I had never prayed before. My prayer life had shifted. I was praying off generational curses and blood line curses because Satan can't have anything or be connected to me, in Jesus' name.

I'm writing this book to show I had to fight before I came to Christ. After coming to Christ, I still have to fight. I got haters that don't even know why they are hating. When I was in the world, they hated me because I was a part of a different gang, I had a man they wanted, or they were just flat out jealous and didn't like me because of my swag.

It's a whole other ball game in the church world. I had cliques in the world, and there are cliques in the church. You have to really know who you are and whose you are because people will mess you up. They get a little control, and they run with it. If you don't act a certain way, dress a certain way, or if you don't have certain titles, you just don't fit all the way in. You can come in, but only so far. You know how the politics run. Yea, it's going down in the church house, yes the house of God.

If you're not a family member of the church leaders, there are certain guidelines you have to follow. You have to go through all the red tape. I've seen certain people go right under the tape. This is not a flesh and blood race because flesh and blood will not inherit the kingdom of God. Some leaders want their physical family to be saved. I understand that because we all do, but once they get them to accept Christ, they begin to pamper them. They give them titles and put them in high positions only to cause a great disaster. They put them in positions because they are used to them and comfortable. But, when you come to Christ, we are new creatures forgetting those which are behind. Our lives and family members can be the fall of us if we're not careful.

If we trust God, we have to trust Him all the way, even when He sends you someone that you just don't want to receive. You know He sent them, but you continue to hold them down and raise the ones up that you are comfortable with. You are trusting in your comfort zone and not God. You're not using the faith that God has given you. In that, you are only hindering your ministry and causing a lot of damage to God's sheep. God said that He paid a high price for their lives and to be very careful how you handle them, for it is better to wrap a millstone around your neck than to harm one of His children.

Ministry is not a physical family affair, for we all are God's children. I have witnessed some stuff over these twenty years in church. I remember one sister in the beginning told me who I was. God showed her what I am supposed to do, but she fought me tooth and nail. She told me one day, "Ain't nobody gone come between me and mines." She was all in my face and yelling and probably spitting a little too. I told her that this is not a flesh and blood battle but a spiritual one. That's all I had in me, and I believe I told her, "If you want to yell and act undignified, I can go there, but I choose not to." I've had sisters that told me they don't know why but it's just something about me to where they can't receive me. Another sister would smile in my face and act like she loved you, but put all kind of daggers in my back.

When you first go to a new church, the ones that are there before you automatically get defensive. They feel like you are there to move them out of their positions. In reality, you should be. That's the way it should go. Don't be so stuck and used to a position to where you don't want to move. If you are in right standing, the only way to move is upward. You get your eyes off of God and His people and become focused on the title, the position and the pastors, sad to say.

Sometimes, I would have a decent and regular conversation with one of my sisters, and she would turn it around and take it to the pastor. It would always turn on me. A sister would say, "Is everything okay? You can talk to me if there is a problem." She would practically beg me to talk. When I went for it, she would flip out and then hurry up and talk to the pastors. It was a mess and would always say it's not a one-man show, but she had to run the whole show and wouldn't want any of my advice. She got what she thought she needed, but she needed so much more.

In the world, they will rob you and steal from you. It's in the church too. Even in Malachi it asks, "Will a man rob God?" He said, "Yes, in tithes and offering." So, if they steal from God, what do you think they think about you? Some churches only see you as tithes and offerings. I know it's sad. I've seen the leaders allow their blood family to get away with things that they wouldn't dare allow the rest to get away with. But thank God I wasn't one of them. I earned everything. I got even the lies, scandal, back biting, etc. It pushed me into my destiny. I have learned a lot in the ministries that I've been with, but I've also learned a lot of what not to do.

I'm not sharing my experiences with you to say I'm never going to church. No, of course not. I'm telling you so you can be prepared when you get there. So you will know what you're up against. I felt like I was deceived. I believe that God is bringing in the remnant of people that is counted out, a people that won't be easily stroked, one that won't compromise, one that knows that it was God that saved them and snatched them out of the hand of hell. I know some people that treat God's people like their puppets. God will give you shepherds after His own heart, but sometimes you want to serve them as your leaders here on earth, but people allow flesh and elevation to take their positions out of context.

There is another reason I wasn't liked too much. They said I always had something to say, but there had to be an objective somewhere if we all are listening to one person and going in one direction. We seem to keep going around and around and not moving nowhere. Somebody needs to be able to say something because I feel like if there were more people like me to ask questions during the Jim Jones' episode, it probably could have turned out differently. That's one reason why they call some churches occults because they do their own thing. They operate in the spirit of control. They have a controlling spirit and don't even know it.

No one but God should have that much control over a person, and even He gave people a self will. People should be allowed to have their own mind. I thought when I got saved it would be all good, but not so. The devil really raised the heat on me. It's pretty sad that He can use your spiritual siblings to do it. Make sure you're not one of the haters, but a congratulator. If you're reading this book, and it seems like you fall short in that area, get delivered. Don't be on both teams!

Chapter Seven

My Sonflower and The Great Betrayal

Anthony May, Jr.

MY SONFLOWER, you are a flower that I really don't have enough words for. I know that you are full of life. You are a multi-tasker. You're strong and can stand alone. But when accompanied by others, you shine even more because of who you are and who you're called to be. There is so very much connected to you. If I were you, I would just go ahead and do exactly what our father tells you to do. You are rare. You're not common, and you will never fit in. The "in" will fit in you. Not only are you beautiful, but you produce substance. It's in you. There is a seed in you that many people need. Don't be afraid, and don't be dismayed. Don't allow the enemy's pesticides to damage or destroy you. You are far too valuable to our Lord and Savior. Allow God to plant you in a healthy environment. So you can be fed, nourished and cultivated, so that you may grow and flourish. And the seed in you can be activated. Out of that one seed, God will produce many seeds. So, be who God created you to be: healthy and wealthy, in Jesus' name. You shall proclaim and remember the scripture: the more you give, the more will be given to you, pressed down, shaken together will men give into your bosom. Love, Mommy.

I had always wanted a son from the very first time I had conceived. It took three girls, and then came my boy. The bible says to whom much is given, much is required, and my boy is a bit much. That came from a relationship of abuse, hurt, and pain, and to top it off from being in an unequally-yoked marriage. I was twenty-five years old, and I was really feeling myself by then. My girls were at the age where they could look out for one another without the law getting involved.

One day, I had gone to my long-time friend's house. I was talking to her and her dude, inquiring and whining about a TV. I wanted to purchase from them. Her boyfriend had just sold it. Guess who walked in? Mr. Man. He came in very strong and convincing, by asking me for my phone number so he could buy me a new TV. I shot him down immediately, and replied, "I don't think so. I'm not taking any new applications right now." That's crazy. I know. At that time, I had a guy for sex, another for money, and one that was pleasing on the eyes. So, I didn't felt like had any room for anyone else in my life. I was set because I was taking care of my girls by myself. I didn't need a Negro to ever think my girls owed him nothing.

Let's get back to Mr. Man. He was very persistent, and so was I. It wasn't going down. At least, so I thought. As I was leaving and approaching my car, he followed me and said, "By any chance if you really need that TV give me a call." Then, he offered me his phone number still not knowing at that time he was packing my son (LOL). Time went on, and somehow I got bored, so I gave him a call. We went to the movies, out to eat, and to have cocktails. We hung out together a lot, but he never bothered me for sex. I almost thought he was gay, but he was far from that. I found out later he was totally the opposite. Much to my surprise, he was a womanizer, and still is- even to this day. Help him, Lord.

As time moved on, Mr. Mr. Al would always make sure he asked about me. He would say I was his girl and that it was something about me. But, he moved to Texas for about five years because he had gotten on crack cocaine real bad and couldn't take care of himself at all. When he finally got in touch with me, I was doing bigger and better things. I had moved on, but there was a very special place in my heart for him. I was crazy about him.

One day he called me from Texas. I was living in Hawthorne at the time, and I was going out with Mr. Man, but it wasn't too serious, but serious enough. I talked to Mr. Al everyday for about four to six months. He ran up his dad's phone bill up really high. We didn't have cell phones like we do today. He had a good job working with his dad doing construction, but after he had been speaking with me for so long, he worked long enough to save some money and come back to Cali.

When he got here, I was happy to see him. We went to his family functions and everything. Then, we went to my house and chilled. When the morning came, I asked him, "Where do you want me to drop you off at?" He said, "Nowhere. I'm with you. I came out here to be with you." I said, "I'm on another program. I'm doing me. I've been too tied down for too long. I'm just starting to enjoy my life." By the way, I never did forget when he dumped me in the rain at the phone booth. He wanted to get married at that point, but I said no. He wasn't thug or gangster enough for me. So, he went back to his family and started back using drugs. Then, he went to jail.

Meanwhile, Mr. Man and I started spending more time together, and eventually, I invited him to bed. He still never approached me for sex, to the point where I began to push up against him, hinting to him that it was okay. I let him know, "It's safe. You can have some. You've passed the ninety-day loyalty probation period." I was something else. I had my life mapped to a science when it came to men. But as time went on, we handled our business. He was my twelfth boyfriend. You know, twelve is a number of order. And believe you me, he set the order.

He changed my life all the way around to where the things I used to do I just didn't do them anymore because he wanted me locked in and working at home. It had gotten to a point that he would drop me at work, pick me up and sometimes sit outside my workplace in my car. He wanted to monitor the clients that I had, and he would pay me not to do my male hommies' hair. He would say, "How much are curls?" At that time, the price was $50.00. He would pay that and say, "I don't need all these niggahs in and out of the salon." I was digging on him like that by then, so you know I shut it down. I watched my whole agenda become his agenda. My life began to evolve and fit into his life. I was so sprung.

I had always been afraid of flying, but when he moved part of his business to Arizona, I began to fly every Saturday or Sunday after work. What people do for love. But, I wasn't sprung by myself. Back then, he didn't even want me around my friends or family. He did an operation lock down for real. I remember my girl had come home from being incarcerated. She was a mutual friend of ours. But, he wasn't having us going out together. One day, she came over, and I took her out for her birthday, and she spent the night. He came in the next day and tripped out because we were on our way out again. By then, he had already started becoming abusive.

At that time, he had been shot in his arm and butt, so there he was limping around and telling me I was not going nowhere. He snatched me up, and I must have taken advantage of his weakness. I turned around, grabbed him by his shirt, pushed him against the refrigerator, balled my right fist and was about to let him have it. My girl came in, and said, "Don't do it. Let him go." I did. That was the scene in *The Color Purple* when Oprah beat Harpo.

As time went on, I became pregnant, but I didn't want any more kids. I had given up on my boy. I didn't tell him I was pregnant when I went and had the abortion. He had already warned me if I ever got pregnant that it would be of our decision. So I didn't tell him, but he said my close friend came and told him all about the abortion and about my safety net (where I was hiding names and numbers of my old and new flames under my mattress in the middle of the my bed. That was my rainy day stash.) He flipped up my mattress and went straight to my stash; he started tripping, crying, and acting crazy; he was full of anger and rage. He said, "This isn't over! You killed my baby! I know you did because your friend told me, and I know she wasn't lying." She wasn't.

I didn't even tell you that he was a gangbanger. At that moment, it seemed like he was gangbanging on me. He told me that because I took life and death in my own hands, he was about to do the same thing when it came to me because I had killed his baby. He said, "I'm gone kill you." I was terrified. I had never been known for talking my way out or into something. That moment would have been the perfect time, so I had to do what I had to do. At that point, I had to think real fast. I decided to use it or lose it. I began to tell him that I loved him and how sorry I was and that I was scared to have any more children and be left alone to raise them. I began to make mad crazy love to him. That's all I could do. That's all I knew to do. I guess it worked. I'm still alive today to tell the story. Thank you, Lord.

We continued to be together, and shortly after, he went to jail. I got really serious in church. I had been going, but I was still doing stuff I should not have been doing. So, when he went to jail, it was a relief. I began to minister, teach Sunday school and direct the choir also, for about sixteen months.

While he was gone, I was faithful to him. I didn't cheat on him. All I did was go to work and church. He asked me to marry him when he was in jail. As a matter of fact, he probably didn't ask me. I probably told him that if he wanted to be with me and have some you-know-what, he had to marry me. So, that's what he did.

He got out one week, and within two weeks, we were married. Did I ask God? No. Did I know if he was my husband? No, I didn't wait to see. It was all about sex. I remember when we were living together, and we weren't married. I had gotten saved, but he wasn't. So, he was doing his thing, and I was doing mine. My life began to circle around God more and more. He was still doing the same thing, so the more I got involved in church, the less I would want to come home to him and have sex, curse, argue, and fight. God had made a way of escape when he allowed him to get arrested and do some time. I didn't take heed; instead, I got unequally yoked.

God sent my cousin Kai to ask me if I was sure that I wanted to marry him. She asked me, "Did God tell you that he was your husband?" I simply said, "I don't know, and I am hard of hearing anyway." That wasn't true. I was full of flesh and compromising. I was holding onto the scripture where Paul says that it is better to marry than to burn. But with what I went through in my marriage, I could have burned for eternity. In the first year, I got pregnant, and my husband and I said that was my honeymoon baby.

In all honesty, if I can keep it real and get free at the same time, I gave him some the second night when he came home just to try and hold him off for a little while until we got married. Honey please, let me tell it. He got hooked up on the first day by someone else when he came home. You know my self esteem was so low that I pretty much settled for anything.

Looking back on some things, when we had to move, he would wait right up to the point when I had to move or get evicted and he would leave. I would work, make the money, find the place, and move me and my kids. Low and behold, shortly after, he would come easing on in. Shame on me.

I was worth so much more, but I settled for so much less. Remember this, a man or anyone will only do what you allow him to do to you. When you're in a relationship with someone, he/she is going to either add or subtract. When you are confident in yourself and know your worth, you just won't take no less than the best.

As time went on, I was pregnant with my son, and I was still going to church. Everywhere I would go, the prophets and the preachers would say that I was carrying a mighty man of God, an ordained minister, and that he would preach the gospel. They were more accurate than the ultrasound.

When I was about seven or eight months pregnant, I wanted my husband to stay with me to do something. He didn't want to, and he started to struggle with me. He threw me on the bed and was pretty much sitting on me. One of my daughters came in with a bat and told him to get off her mama. I guess he could see the seriousness in her eyes. She was about to knock his head off. He got up and left. I was miserable because I felt like I married him, and I was having another baby. I just didn't want to go through having another child and raising him on my own because all of my three daughters' dads never came to the hospital when they were born. So, I tried everything I could to hold onto my husband.

When time came to have the baby, he took me to the hospital in a low rider down Alameda. It was a bumpy ride, but as long as I was with him, it was like rolling in a limousine in Beverly Hills. When we got to the hospital, he said, "Yea, I'm gone be right there when my son is born. I done seen all kind of stuff on the streets, so that's nothing."

As soon as the doctor said it was time to go in the delivery room and handed the mask and gown to him, he was so scared and didn't know what to do. My cousin Charlotte was there. He handed it over to her. She was there to see my son come out, and she cut the cord.

That really meant a lot to me. Thank you, cousin. You separated my son from me when he came into the world, and I hope through God's mercy and grace, you will allow God to use me as a vessel to help detach you from your son now that he has left this world. I love you and respect you, but I would never want to be in your shoes and go through what you've been through. You are so strong. I commend and salute you. May the Lord continue to keep you in Jesus' name.

As time went on, my husband and I just couldn't seem to get it together. I would go to church and come home, and he would be at home drinking or smoking. I also remember the times when the kids and I would go to church, and when we came home, he would have a full-course meal ready. I would be so happy until I got to the kitchen. There would be corn meal and flour all over the whole kitchen, even on the ceiling.

I'm not saying all our issues were entirely my husband's fault because I had my share of the blame too. I would nag him and argue and would insist on talking even though he didn't want to. There were times when I would start fights. I remember if I didn't get my way with him, we would fall out. It would mess my whole day up, and I would say, "I'm not going to church." That was until God asked me what my husband has to do with my praise and my worship. "Did you wake up this morning? Did I keep you and your family safe? Did I feed you today? Have I been faithful to you in spite of whom and how you've been to me?" All I could do was repent. It had gotten so bad that I started preaching, He gave me a message on worshipping the creature more than the creator.

I feel like whomever you are spending more time with is your God. Whomever you go to sleep thinking about and wake up thinking about is your God. We may say one thing, like "God is first and the head of my life," but all I can say is, "Please, don't be deceived." Some people's jobs can be their God. Your kids, your money, your lover, your husband or wife, or whatever or whomever you find yourself meditating and spending more time on instead of God. He is supposed to be our highest priority. If only we would allow Him to reign in our lives, our lives would be so much better.

In the first year of my marriage, my son was born and my husband was going back and forth out of town. One day, I received my telephone bill. I found myself digging through it. The bible says seek and you shall find. I looked on the number from the calling card, and I began to dial a phone number. The girl who answered told me what I wanted to hear. The next and last call was a hot one.

I dialed the number, and I said, "Hello, this is Katrina. I found your number on my phone bill that was placed with our calling card." I asked her if she knew Man, and I believe she said no. Then, I said, "Well, do you know Anthony?" She said, "Yes." She said that he was her fiancé, and then she asked me who I was. I told her that I was his wife. She screamed and dropped the phone as if someone had died. Then, her cousin picked up the phone and began speaking with me. I asked her to put the young lady back on the phone. She did, and as we began to talk, she said she wished that I would have called her about seven or more months earlier because she was seven months pregnant. That's when my heart dropped, and my stomach became full of butterflies.

It was good for him that he was out of town. He had time on his side, but it was horrible for me. The young lady and I continued to talk. We came up with a plan to catch him right in his act. So, when he would call, I would talk to him like nothing had ever happened, but was cutting me deeper and deeper.

The plan was for us to wait for him to come back home and to wait for him to go to her house. Then, she would call me and put me on the phone. She did that, and when he heard me on the other line, I believe he could have used the bathroom on himself. He was so scared and such a coward that he did everything but come home to deal with the situation. He ran right to his mother's house, and I finally went over there and caught him outside talking to his cousins. I confronted him and pleaded with him to come home so we could talk. I don't know what I wanted to hear. I guess one of his great spectacular lies, but he didn't want to deal with it like a man and a married man at that.

He began to struggle with me and pushed me up against the car. His cousin said, "Man, won't you go home and deal with your wife." His cousins broke the fight up. Then, his mom came outside and walked across the street. For one minute I thought that she would be compassionate for me, but the words that came out of her mouth blew me back. She told him, "I told you in the first place. I told you not to marry her." She always took his side. She never accepted me until we were separated. To this day, I feel like I was the best thing that could have ever happened to him.

I knew his mother didn't want him to marry me because she didn't get the family's clothes for our wedding until the wedding day. She was in complete denial. She took it as if when we got married she would be losing a son. But she should have taken it as she was gaining another daughter. She never taught me how to be a wise woman, to build my house instead of tearing down. Yes, she gave me a few recipes and would tell me to make sure I kept the house clean. But I feel like she never thought I was good enough for her son. Yes, I had three kids, but I held my own. I thank God that we have Him because I love my mother-in-law to this day.

Even before the other woman, I should have known something was really wrong. Our marriage was over after I had the baby. One day, he gave me money to get my hair and nails done. But I was gone too long for him. He kept calling me. When I finally got home, his brother told me that he was mad, but I didn't know how mad. I went in my room and told him that I was going out with some friends from the salon. I was looking GQ.

He said, "No, you're not." I said, "I never go anywhere. All I do is go to work and church. I'm going to *The Laugh Factory*." I got in the shower and got dressed. I picked my baby up and was kissing him, probably saying bye. He told me again, "Man, I told you. You not going nowhere." I said, "Yes, I am."

All of a sudden, he hit me so hard I saw stars. He had never in life hit me that hard. I didn't have no get back. I think I had my baby in my hands. I fell on the bed and grabbed a pillow. I just knew all my front teeth were knocked out. Immediately, he said, "I'm sorry. I did not mean to hit you that hard. I am so sorry." He got me a towel, and he took me to the hospital. The nurses and the doctor were trying to get me to tell them what had really happened, but I didn't.

That night, he said he hit me with an opened back hand and that he did not ball his fist. I beg to differ. I had been slapped before and you know back in the day, they called that a pimp slap. It ain't no telling; they probably still do. He hit me so hard that he chipped over half of one of my front teeth and chipped a third of the other one. One of them is still loose in my head. One thing I do know for sure is that he hit me so hard that he knocked all the love out of me. There is no way he could love me and hit me like that.

When I got back from the hospital, I asked him to leave. He said that was cool, but the longer he was gone, he would have his brother and sisters tell me how bad he was looking and how bad he was doing without me and the kids. He said he was really depressed, so he asked if he could come back. Me being a dumbo, I let him come back. When he came back, he just couldn't believe that he could have a good and faithful wife with him being a lousy husband to me.

As time went on, I started going out. Once, I went to a friend's birthday party and came in too late. The next morning, he woke up and called me whores and sluts. He talked about me coming in at motel booty-call hours, but at that time, I was still faithful to my husband. It was one thing for him to tear me down, but it was another to do it in broad daylight and loud enough for my girls to hear him.

I wanted to give my girls a chance. I knew that it was a strong chance that if my girls witnessed him physically and verbally abusing their mom that they, later in life, could be victims. They may think, *if it's good enough for mama, it's good enough for me.* The fruit don't fall too far from the tree.

That's when I told him to leave and don't ever come back. For one, the love was already gone, and the respect for me and my kids was gone. So he needed to be gone out of our lives. I knew I was in denial. Someone had his heart, and it was no longer me. (As I wrote this chapter, I was finally able to get some closure.)

As time went on, the other woman felt like she wanted my husband, but he wanted us both. It wasn't going down on my clock, so I gave up on my marriage shortly after. Have I had regrets? Yes, most definitely. I feel like I gave up too soon. I have had plenty of lonely days and night. I've been in full-time ministry, but yet I have felt empty and incomplete.

The other woman had the baby; it was a girl. I was broken, so I began to drink. I stopped going to church, and I was mad at everybody. I guess that included God because when I left my husband, I left God too.

When I went over to my mother-in-law's, the baby was there. I would call her a little illegitimate 'b,' and I know it was not the child's fault. As time went on, I went back to God. The baby got older, and she began to grow on me. God softened my heart. She went from being my illegitimate 'b' to my illegitimate stepdaughter to my stepdaughter to my daughter. God is good.

Later, my husband moved in with the other woman, and she had a baby boy shortly after. They thought they would live happily after all, but it didn't happen. She went through hell with him, and he's still going through it. He had a baby on her, and she went crazy from him cheating on her. I remember that old saying 'what's good for the goose is good for the gander.'

As I look back, it seemed like he never loved me, but how could he when he didn't love God or himself? The day we got married was the last time he walked into a church unless he went to a funeral. I know that's bad on my behalf also because the bible says a sanctified wife can save her husband. I failed. I didn't pass the test. It was one test after another, and I was flunking back to back. I didn't have any of the mothers of the church or the older or more mature men and women of God to encourage me or help me out.

When I found out my husband had another woman carrying his child, I was so ashamed and embarrassed. I thought I was the first and the last that that had ever happened to. Oh, but I was so wrong. Would I do it all over again? I couldn't say that I would, but if it would help somebody so that they don't have to go through it, then maybe. Some women from where I came from didn't make it through it. They were killed in the midst of an abusive relationship.

Know who you are. If you don't know who you are, find out who you are and whose you are. Don't settle for nothing less than the best.

When I left him or he left me, I was broken, hurt and disgusted. I signed up for it when I didn't go before the Lord and wait on God to give me the go ahead. I was at home alone once again with another kid. I remember when my husband wanted to leave me with that very son that I wanted so bad. I hung my son over my balcony by his legs and told him, "You forgot something. You not leaving me with him by myself." I didn't plan on hurting my son, but I gave the enemy some leverage over my situation. He could have slipped out of my hands and broke his neck or even been killed. I give all glory to God. He didn't allow that to happen. Thank you, my Lord.

Another time when his dad and I had gotten into it, he was riding with his homeboys, and I popped up over his mom's. His car was parked down the street with a girl in it. I was talking to him, so that I could get the money for the rent. He would always have me in an awkward position when it came to my rent and bills. That's why I'm an independent black woman. We were standing in the street, and I knew something smelled fishy, but I couldn't afford to trip out on him right then.

I really needed to pay my rent, so there he was standing in the street talking mess. I was taking it because he told his sister Pat to go and get the money for me. She also had my baby too. He said something, and I saw a girl in his car. All I did was slap him so hard to where they heard it at his aunty's house, which was past the middle of the block. He said, "You crazy." His sister Pat was coming to the door with the money, and he said, "Don't give her you-know-what, Pat." I was very persistent back then. I stayed around and kissed up to him until he forgave me. I got my money from him and that was it for the night.

He wasn't always bad and selfish. I believe that's all he knew. He didn't know how to be a good and devoted husband because he never had anyone to teach him or lead him by example. He was so worried about his reputation with his homeboys. That caused him to lose. He was so worried about what they thought about our relationship than him trying to make the best out of what we had. None of those so-called friends are around today.

He is not a dead-beat dad when it comes to his kids. He will provide and do the best he can. He just needs to open his line of communication because without communication, no relationship can be healthy. Sad to say, he was a much better dad than husband.

One time, I went over there to see him. I was with my cousin and his sister had my baby. We got into a fight because he was showing off in front of his friend. After we got into it, I went to get my baby from his sister. She was right at the door, and he told her take him in the house and not to give me my baby. That's exactly what she did. She would do whatever he told her to do. She rolled with her brother for sure. When I got my baby later, it was awhile before they saw him again.

The only one that had my back was my sister-in-law Wanda. When I moved, I moved on to Long Beach. I was blessed with low-income housing for a period of time. I worked like a dog, and in the process of the hurt and pain, I backslid or as the world would say slid backwards. I started back drinking and partying. I would drink and drive home. My oldest would be waiting up for me until I came in, no matter what time I came in. Sometimes, I didn't come in until the next day.

There were times when we would be in the living room chilling and playing with their baby brother. I had bought him a little crown and scepter. I had a horrible little saying that I would make them bow down and say when they made him mad: "Sorry, king master lord Jr." I know I was sick, but we were all delivered from that. Jr's deliverance isn't complete yet. When he was about seven or eight years old, God came to me and told me that nobody wants nothing that's spoiled and rotten in their presence. They do whatever they can do to get away.

Just imagine if you had something rotten in your house. You don't put it in the trash in the house. You put it outside the house, and you can't wait for the trash man to come and get it off your premises, especially if there are maggots around. At that point, I began to ease up on spoiling him. It wasn't easy but it came from God. I know He wasn't leading me wrong.

As time went on, Jr. got a little older. When he was around thirteen, the Lord took me to the scripture where He said that if I do not discipline him, I don't love him and that I could cause him to lose his life. If I discipline him and lead him down the right path, life would be added to his life.

When he was younger, he loved church. He loved to sing and preach, but the older he got, the less he wanted to preach and sing for Jesus. I never had a problem with him in school other than him thinking the teachers were supposed cater to him like me and his sisters. He had to learn fast because I told him that it is a great big world out there, and it doesn't revolve around him. I gave him so much; I have gone out of my way like crazy. I told him that it was going to be very hard for him to get a good woman and keep her because he has been so used to being in a seventy-thirty relationship. He barely gives thirty in our relationship.

He treated me so bad at times. He always wants to challenge me at any given time. He takes his time to do what I say, but when it comes to his dad, he may feel one way about him but he would never let anyone talk about him and would take up for him at the drop of a dime. He has always respected his dad no matter what. I don't know if it is a man thing or what.

As Anthony grew older, he became more opinionated and stubborn. As he got older, he got bigger and more hard headed, so I would find myself calling his dad. Most of the time, his dad would turn it against me and actually curse me out. If I tried to whip him his dad would get so upset that he would sound like he was getting a whipping. When his eighteenth birthday was approaching, his senior social, prom, grand night, graduation and a new car were supposed to jump off. I told his dad about everything, and instead of him being happy and proud, all he could say is, "I'm gone tell you right now I don't got no money." That surprised me, but I was used to him having me carry the load alone.

I must admit his reaction jolted me a little because that's his boy. I know he loves him, and in spite of everything Jr. is not a bad kid. They come much worse. I have never had to worry about him gang banging, other than Facebook banging. I didn't worry about him hanging out, selling drugs or messing with a lot of little fast-tail girls, at least not yet. As a matter of fact, he won't sell drugs, in Jesus' name.

I would like to thank Mr. Man for not fighting against me when our son was growing up by trying to insist that he come to his house in L.A. I have to admit he has first cousins around the same age as he is, and they live a much more advanced life. I remember the time when I came into my husband's life, and his nephews were so much younger. As time went on, my mother-in-law had not only raised her children and their outcome was drugs, alcohol, and gang banging, but she also raised the grandkids. As time went on, it was drug dealing and hard gang banging for them too.

I remember telling their mother a few times that she should keep her own kids and to take them and keep them where she lived. She tried, but eventually she gave in and allowed them to go and stay on the east side with their granny. Both of her sons have life in jail and my sister-in-law drunk herself to death and that hurt my heart. The whole family has taken a great loss. My point is that I am watching history repeat itself. She is now raising my grandson, but really her motherhood season is up. She should just play the role of a granny, even though she is doing it from her heart. She means well, but it's not for the good of the kids.

She used to keep my son when he was a baby and through his toddler years. He was and still is a granny's boy, but I had to pull him out so that he could have a chance in life by not being caught up in gang banging and drinking like crazy and doing drugs. I'm not judging his family to be all negative or anything because they have a ninety percent success rate in graduating from high school. My son will be the first out of this generation to go to college and complete it. He will take it to a higher level. I don't mean no harm, but it is what it is and it do what it do.

The grandkids before his generation have pretty decent jobs and their own places. They are dependable. I love all of them. They're my family. They have accepted me over the years. My sister-in-law Wanda loved me from the beginning. She would call me 'legal'- even to this day. There were times when I was in transition and needed a place to stay. She allowed me to come and stay with her, and she fed us. She also gave me a key to her place. She never mistreated me or my kids. As soon as she knew my situation, she opened her home to me, and she always had my back even when her brother would be doing the do. She would find some kind of way to let me know something so I wouldn't look like a complete fool because I did look like a fool for sure.

When my husband cheated on me and got the other woman pregnant, she was coming around to his mom's house and his sister's. I didn't know nothing about it. She should have been so far in the cut, it wouldn't make sense. Eventually, she came out and about, and I faded away. But, they both had hell to pay. He did the same thing to her that he did to me, and she just couldn't deal with it. She went crazy on him and left him and the kids. Now, he's the housewife. I'm talking cooking, washing clothes, cleaning, and taking the kids to school. When he had me, I did it all, even wash his tail when I had to.

I remember when he lost all his money and had his mom to borrow on her house. When he got the money, I asked him to invest in our business. I had already had a hair salon, and I wanted to expand and open a beauty supply inside my salon. But, he said I had to wait. What he did do was invest it in you know what, and the deal went bad. He lost everything, and he was a sick puppy dog. I went in my stash and gave it all to him. Yes, I was a ride-or-die chick. I was with him when he had and when he lost everything, I helped him come up. It be like that sometimes.

When we had broken up, it was bad at first. He paid the rent that last month, and I didn't want to see him for several months. When I began to let him see our son, he began to help us financially. He started with giving us between five hundred and eight hundred dollars. Then, he went to four hundred. Shortly from there, it went back to nothing other than him buying our son clothes and shoes and giving him a little pocket change. I guess something is better than nothing because my other kids' dads didn't do anything for them. Latrina's dad didn't do for her until she was sixteen. Casanova always took care of my kids, and when we broke up, he still took care of her as if she was his biologically.

It never set well with me that Mr. Man could leave his wife and kids. Do he leave us for dead? The rent still needed to be paid, we still needed lights, and we still needed to eat. If he didn't want to pay alimony, what about child support? He is still responsible to make sure his child has a place to live not just the kids that live with him. It felt like out of sight out of mind.

During our son's senior year of high school, and he told us that he would pay for the senior package. But, on the day he was to give the money, he gave him less than half of what was due. I had already told him that I wouldn't be able to cover him and take care of it. I hadn't been able to work because my mom was in the hospital. We were so disappointed that we didn't say anything. So, we just left. I had to ask the people that my son and I were bragging to about how he said that he was going to take care of all of it to help out. They did the best they could. Some had it and didn't give. Another just simply ignored the situation.

So, I waited a couple of days. I prayed, and I asked my son if he wanted to call or go and ask his dad for the rest of the money. He said no he didn't want to ask him for nothing. So, I had to pray, and I went for it. He tried to turn me down. Then, he tried to tell me that he would send it to us later on that day. I just stood there. I spoke when I as led, but for the most, I was quiet but determined and persistent. He went to the back and came and handed me the rest of the money.

I had been through so much that week. The enemy was trying to attack us, but we held onto God's unchanging hand. Satan can't do nothing that God don't allow him to do. Everything He does to me makes me stronger and stronger and pushes me closer and closer to my destiny. As long as I'm in the will of God and I'm in the plan that God has ordained over my life, then I know that not only will I be blessed with heaven's best, but my family will be also.

I was sick that whole weekend. On Friday, we missed my son's senior meeting, and I just found out that it was mandatory in order for him to walk across the stage. I called the school counselor and before I knew it. I broke. I began to explain to him what I've been through the last week, and I began to cry. Before I knew it, the teacher was praying for me and my family.

I had been waiting twelve years for this time, and there I was dropping the ball. The devil is a liar. The favor of God is upon our lives, and I like it like that. Monday took forever to come. But, thank God, it came. When we got to the school, the head counselor was already there waiting for us and had already talked to a couple of people on our behalf. Everything worked out. We didn't even have all the money, but God worked it out for us to have almost two extra weeks to pay. I thank God for that because He knows I hadn't been able to work with being in L.A. taking care of my mom and God's business and all. So at that point, it was on my son. He had to make sure he got all of his credits, so he could walk across that stage.

I went back into the city, and we were waiting got my mom's test results to come back. They finally came in, and it wasn't the report we wanted to hear. The doctors said the Cancer had come back, and it was in her airway. But, I knew whose report I was going to believe. It was the report of the Lord. I proclaimed, "She's healed, she's free, and she got the victory in Jesus' name." I was there to do what God called me to do. I needed to take good care of my mom and my family. I had been separated from them for so long, but I knew God had sent me back to my family to help draw them to Him. My family seemed ripe. They were hungry for God. They wanted God. They just didn't know how to get Him. I believe it was my job to help them because the bible says that ministry starts at home.

That weekend, I ministered at a prayer breakfast, and God showed up and showed out. I didn't believe I could do it, but it was God that did it. While I was ministering, I was preaching to myself. God had me to preach from the book of Joel, dealing with how He had allowed the locusts to devour the land. What had happened had never happened and never will happen again. In our families, we are experiencing something that we have never been through, like death in our family. In my family, it was our niece first, who at that time was the youngest in our family. Then, it was my dad, who was the oldest in our family. Then, it hit the middle age generation. I know it's only God trying to get our attention.

I was able to push and deliver the message, and God came with a rhema prophetic word for me. He said that my mother will live a long time and that she would be fine and that the fire of the Lord was upon me. I was going to a higher level. This word came from a Caucasian older man that came upon me so quickly to where I had to block him.

But he came with a certain boldness to where I didn't want to stop my blessings. I believe he is an end-time prophet. God's prophets are not the ones who allow the spirit of intimidation to grip them or the ones that are so arrogant with their gift. Don't forget about the false prophets who just want to have a word, but it's not a word from the Lord. I thank God for the obedience and boldness that the man and women of God operated in on March 31, 2012.

Right after the prophet had spoken, a woman of God came over to me and said that I will speak internationally. She said because of my obedience with delivering that particular word, God was pleased. She said He told her to salute me in the name of the Father, the Son, and the Holy Spirit. She touched my belly and declared a healing right where I had been paining for a long time. Before I could leave, another woman of God in red told me that she did not want to say anything to me with everybody around me. She was waiting for her friend to come out of the restroom, so they could go and visit a sister in the hospital, but God kept dealing with her. So, she came over to me and said that God told her that I will be going so much higher and that my book is going to be a movie and to continue to speak just the way He tells me to. Then, she said that I will be able to move and live wherever I choose to and that God is going to give me a blank check. When I got in the car, my sister said that God had told her that same thing in His word. We were so overwhelmed. As you can see, all of the prophets complimented each other, without hearing one another. They were vessels for God. I am so grateful for their obedience.

For the next couple of days, I took care of my mom, and I went to my sister's. A couple of my niece's friends came over, one of whom I mentored. When she began to leave, she said, "I'll see you later." She put something in my hand and blessed me. I prayed and blessed her for sowing into my life. You see, no one knew that I didn't have any more money. I didn't even know how I was going to get home. I mean, I had really been walking by faith. God had been meeting every need. Thank you, my Lord. You see all can't call Him their Lord because He's not the Lord over their lives.

I had to tell my sisters and brothers one by one that it's going to take more than just me to sacrifice, but all of us. This was the twelfth year that our mom had been healed from Cancer, but then it was back. Twelve is a number of order, and it was time for order. It had been twelve years since God showed me my destiny, and I had begun to pursue it. It is the year 2012, and twelve just happens to be God's number. My heart beat is twelve years old, yes Damone. He has a very special place in my heart. I love all my grands, and they all love me. They all have their own part of me.

I have been through so much with Damone. He is another one that's kind of spoiled. I said kind of because he's being delivered right now. I remember his first birthday when we really didn't have any money, and God worked another miracle. He had so many clothes and toys and lots and lots of love. Then came my Naomi. I call her my new and improved Naomi Campbell. She is so beautiful. Shortly after, my Nay came, my white girl. Then came my Tony who loves God and going to church. He taught us another way to worship Jesus. He says,

"Halé, Jesus." Then came my and Mila's Mini-Me- Katrina. She's named after me and has my strong character, but she has her mom's strong features. She loves God and ministry. She's my armor bearer.

Let's take a journey back in time.

There was a time when I was separated from my husband, and I started back drinking, and I stopped going to church. I found myself in the hood at our park celebrating the day my cousin, who I raised like my niece, was killed on July 7. I never would have gone there in my right state of mind because I remember telling my family that you just don't do that. But, I went. From there, they were saying they were going to a hotel function. All my nieces got in the car with me. They were all so much younger than I was. I had absolutely no business having those young girls with me. My niece whose life we were celebrating was with her aunty and big cousins when she got killed. I was mad because I didn't like them letting the young one hang out and do what they did just to kick it. Two years later, I found myself in an even worse situation.

As we were driving down Manchester towards the hotel, Lady Q was contemplating if she was going to go to the hotel or go home to her brand new baby who was only one month old. She asked Cash for some change. She wanted to call and check on her baby, but Cash didn't have any change on her. So, she asked her to give her the purse that was around her neck. We were trying to catch the liquor store which was only a few blocks from her house. My God, the decisions we make. One of my nieces went into the store and the other two and I stayed in the car. A woman came to the window and asked for money. I was talking to her and gave her some money. I have always been very careful at this liquor store. I would say to whoever went there with me to get what you want and let's get out. But, on this night I was just kicking it with no worries in the world. What I'm about to tell you changed my whole world.

As I was talking to the woman on the side of my window, my radio was up. All I heard was my niece behind my seat tell me, "Aunty Trina, they shooting. They shooting." I didn't know what to do. I looked over and put my car in gear. I saw a black guy standing in the middle of the street shooting like cowboys and Indians. My niece Lady Q said, "Trina, I'm hit. I'm hit," with a soft voice. I can still hear her voice. I pulled off, and she said it again. When I was driving up the street, my other niece was holding her and crying and praying and talking to her. So, I pulled over to the first phone booth, and my niece jumped out and dialed 911. I said, "Never mind. I'll drive her. Get in." She got in, and I jumped on the freeway at the next block and went straight to Martin Luther King. They took her right to surgery. We did not see no blood nowhere, but she was bleeding internally, and she didn't make it.

It was a nightmare. I am so sorry for her and for her family, especially her sister and her son. I repent to them for my actions. We shouldn't have been there. One bad move can change your whole world and several people's lives as well. I'm sorry for our loss.

The homicide police came and took us in for questioning. One of the officers told me that we could have been in the middle of crossfire.

They said there was a car behind us that could have been shooting at the guy in the streets that was shooting. Then, the other officer said that he believes that the guy in the street was shooting directly at us, a car full of girls. What a crying shame. He said that if the bullets didn't kill us all, one of the bullets was one centimeter from the gas tank, and it could have blown the car up.

When I was sitting in the car, when he first started shooting, I froze. I saw an angel that blocked me. It was real big and grayish. His wings were like steel. It was my angel of life. I used to minister to Lady Q and all the girls. Lady Q was one of the only ones that had begun to change. I believe she had gotten into some trouble and was on house arrest. All she would do was listen to the gospel channel. God used me to plant the seed; then, the radio station watered it, and God added the increase. On that night, she had a fresh perm, a fresh set of nails and her feet done like she was prepared for her home going. I do know this- if I would have left that night, in hell I would have lifted my eyes. I was a back slider, and my other niece was a mess too. Lady Q was the purest soul that was in the car that night, and I believe she made it into heaven. My niece said she saw her spirit go up.

That was the same day and month five years later, going to the same function, that my other niece was killed. She was pregnant, and they were really close. Five years later, another one of their friends had a baby girl and that curse was broken at that time. When she was killed, I almost lost my mind. I thought about her every day, and then my mom had a heart attack.

I drove all the way to Atlanta, Georgia to check on my mom. When I got back, my sister had been clean from drugs for several years. She had had twins, but she had never had a birthday party for them. I had already told her that I would do it for her, so it was still on the schedule. When I got back from the Atlanta, the party was the next day or two. We handled it, but the day after, my body shut down. I got so sick to where I couldn't move. Every bone in my body was in major pain. I had to lie on my couch and crawl to the restroom for days.

My girls were walking around me and wouldn't help me. They were talking about I was faking. My son was with his granny. He came home after church that Sunday, and he said, "Mama, you don't look good. What's wrong? You sick?" I told him, "Yes, son. Mommy is very sick. I don't feel good at all." He was only about five years old. I asked him if he could pray and lay hands on me. So, he did. When he laid his hands on my head, I began to feel my head and body cool down because I was burning up. I led him through the prayer, and I really began to feel better.

When Monday came, I called my little cousin Na Na to come and take me to the doctor. She came, and I could barely walk. The doctor ran all kinds of tests. They were so puzzled over a woman so young having so many problems with my every joint in my body. The doctor came in and diagnosed me with Lupus. I was devastated. She said that my body was attacking itself. She said my organs were like foreigners, and my body had begun to attack them. They told me that there was one more test that would guarantee that it was Lupus.

I went home, and I think it took the test results about a month to come back. To me, it seemed like a year or a life time. I had to get back to my maker, but I really didn't know how because I was a mess, a real mess. I didn't want to go to Him just because I was in this situation. At that point, it was a couple of days before I went in for my final results. I was at work, and at my job I always shined. I was cocky but humble at the same time. It was around noon, and I went to the restroom and there He was. I thanked Him right now even for me to be in a place to hear Him.

I began to pray; then, He said, "Praise me in advance for your healing." I praised Him. I started out modest, but before I left out of that restroom, I was so loud people were knocking on the door asking me, "Are you fine?" I just said, "Yes." I don't know how long I was in there, but I didn't leave out until I got my break through. After I praised and prayed, I sat on the toilet and a bunch of black bowel came out and filled the whole toilet. I knew at that point I was healed.

A couple of days later, I went to the doctor. They said that I didn't have Lupus. God works like that. He's faithful even when we're not. Thank you, my Lord. But with the damage that was already done in my mind through everything that I had been through over the last year and to have someone tell me that I had a terminal decease and there's no cure, I was gone. I nearly lost my mind. So, when we were taking my new grandbaby to his doctor's appointments, we would talk to his doctor. Then, she started seeing me. She was the one who had diagnosed me; then, she had the nerve to refer me to a therapist. That's really how I felt at the time.

When I met the therapist and began to talk to her, I needed just what the doctor ordered. As I opened up and talked to her, she told me in her line of work, she had noticed that a lot of people and mostly blacks don't want to see a therapist. She said they think that they got to be crazy if they do, but she said, "You're crazy if you don't.' She's a therapist, and she has a therapist as well. She said everybody needs a healthy outlet. When I began to tell her how I was married one year and the next I lost one niece, my husband cheated on me and got another woman pregnant, we were separated, my other niece was killed, my mother had a heart attack and then was diagnosed with Cancer, and I'm the backbone of my family. She said, "The first one to three things you named was enough for you to have had a nervous breakdown." She was surprised that I was functioning the way I was. She commended me for still standing with all that I had gone through.

I told her that I was standing on a solid foundation, not one built by man, but one built by God. It is a spiritual foundation. It is a rock, and the rock is called Jesus. Once you meet Him, I don't care what you go through, you will never be the same. In that season of my life, I was so depressed, suppressed, and oppressed. I didn't know whether I was coming or going. There were times when I would not get out of the bed, wouldn't comb my hair, take a bath or go to church or work. I was completely on shut-down mode.

Where were the saints? I don't know where my family was. I thought I didn't know where God was, but He was right there. He kept my mind. I had a little scripture, and I would speak it. Jesus filled in the rest of the gaps. So, what brought me out? It took God, the therapist, and Zoloft. Yes, Zoloft. I took it for almost a year, until they shut the program down. It was a mild anti-depressant that they prescribed to me. That began to tell my brain to tell my body to get up, comb your hair, wash your face, and you know what else. It gave me strength to clean my house and start back working.

Eventually, I went back to church. It took time because I was church hurt, and you know they say that's the worst hurt. I feel like they left me for dead, but like I said God is faithful. I can't hold that against them or Him because you can't assume that your church members or pastor knows exactly what's going on with you. You have to communicate with them. Whatever didn't kill me made me stronger. And to this day, it is such a powerful testimony. To God be the glory! I have the victory, and He has the glory.

So as time moved on, I had found a place real quick by the grace of God, and we lived there for a while. Shortly after Lady Q passed, my grandbaby was about six weeks old, and he woke up screaming. He had never done that before. It was about 3:15 in the morning, give or take, and my daughter said she felt like something was very wrong. She tried to call his daddy but wasn't successful. Around six or seven in the morning, she got a call from her boyfriend's cousin with the horrifying, devastating, and breath-taking news that he was killed. Yes, my grandson's father. When my daughter got the death certificate later, she said that the time of death was 3:15am. How much more could we take. His death hit us so hard.

It's still hard on us like it was yesterday or maybe a year ago. My daughter is just now trying to regain herself twelve years later from the tragedy. I have been helping her in whatever area I could. I have been helping her in raising my grandson financially, spiritually and emotionally, and don't forget physically. One thing I have always tried to do is keep my word when it came to his shoes to this day. She told me that Lil' Man was crazy about shoes, and he wanted his son to have all kinds of shoes and at least keep him on a clean pair of kicks. So, I told her that I would be responsible for his shoes, and I would take up the slack from his dad. I told her to buy the clothes and I would buy the shoes. We've been working it out ever since. I am a grandson's lady, and he's a granny's baby. I love him so very much, and he knows it. That's why you see you might have caught him and his son fitted; they represented their last name. When it came to their shorts, they knew how to wear them young. He do me like he do me.

We were trying to hold on. It was right around the fourth of July, and I remember telling my family that I didn't like living in the area where I lived with all those fireworks because of the shooting in my car. I was in shell shock. Every time I would hear them, I would literally duck and dodge. My kids and I used to have emergency drills off drive-bys. There was one particular morning around seven or eight, and I was standing in my living room. I heard pop pop pop pop pop pop. I hit the floor, and I yelled, "That ain't no fire crackers this time in the morning." They said, "Calm down, Mama. Yes, it is."

A little time went by, and the neighbors came out of their houses. They said that those sounded like gunshots to them. Then, someone hit the corner and said that a neighbor of ours was shot and killed.

Someone that was there at the wrong time was shot and killed too. That was it.

One day, a woman, whose daughter used to play with my daughter, said she was going out to Rialto to look at some apartments and asked me if I wanted to go. I jumped in her car so fast. We went out there one day. We had washed up all our clothes and packed up. I had started packing the day after the other neighbor was killed. I moved strategically. We had a U-haul and were gone before they could even put him in the ground. Enough was enough. It was time for change. I used to think that I ran from God and my purpose, but I know now I ran to my purpose, and my pain and purpose pushed me into my destiny.

Chapter Eight

My Daisy:
Never Give up Hope

Chloe May

MY DAISY CHLOE, you are my flower that had it rough from the very beginning. You started off so small, feeble and lifeless, but you made it through all types of weather and environments. You have grown in the midst of the wildest weeds that have tried to choke the life out of you. But that couldn't happen because there is a powerful anointed precious gift in you that must be heard across nations. Trust and believe everything that you have been through and everything you're going to go through will be used to glorify God. You shall continue to stand and grow. You were built to stand. Your stems were uniquely designed thick and strong with an automatic protection shield on them. As you grow and blossom, you will stand up strong and tall because you are the baby, and you have the rest of the garden to support and hold you up. So, don't ever give up no matter how bad it looks or gets. Remember, there is always hope as long as your heart still ticks. You are so bright, so beautiful, so full of life, in Jesus Christ. Always remember, Mommy loves you. You shall not die but live and declare the works of the Lord, and you shall live more abundantly.

My baby girl Chloe is my daisy. She feels like no one in the world cares for her, especially not me. It goes back to when she was conceived. She was conceived and born in hurt, pain, rejection, betrayal and depression. Also to top it off, Chloe was conceived when I found out that my husband had cheated on me and had another baby on the way. To top it off, he jumped on me and threw me to the curb.

It didn't kill me, but it broke me to where I started back drinking and you know what else comes with liquor: sex. So, after a four-month stand, I got pregnant, and I had already had four kids. I was by myself too. I just couldn't have another baby. So, I began to handle things the way I used to in the hood. We used abortion as a form of birth control. So, I had my mind made up that I was going to get an abortion. But, my kids didn't want me to. They said that they would keep the baby, and the baby would be their baby. But I said, "I can't have it."

Then, my cousin who thought she couldn't have kids said she would keep the baby. She begged me to keep it, but I was still convinced that I had to abort. So, my cousin told my pastor, and my pastor called me the night before my appointment. She prayed and talked to me for hours, and it was very touching. She said that in spite of everything that I had been through that I was a new creature in Christ, and I couldn't do things the way I used to handle them anymore. When she hung up, and at the end of the day, my mind was still made up. I wasn't having it. Yes, it wasn't a 'her' or a 'him.' I didn't want to make no connection at all.

I went to sleep, and the head honcho came and visited me in a dream or shall I say nightmare. In the dream, I was in the projects. My husband and my third boyfriend, who was a killer and is in jail right now for murder, began to fight. He was getting my husband, and I knew he was going to try and kill him, so I jumped in. I jumped on top of him, and somehow I got a knife. I had my mind made up that I had to kill him because if I didn't, he would kill us all. So, I was stabbing him so many times to where he wasn't moving. I actually over killed him. I was making sure he was dead.

I've never been the type of person to stab or shoot anyone. That wasn't me at all. I looked up for a second, and I saw an ice cream truck. I looked back down, and the guy turned into my one and only pride and joy: my son.

God deals with me in dreams and visions. He told me while I was planning to slaughter this one, He was going to take that one. No one else could convince me, but God knows how to. So, I had the baby, and she was a beautiful girl. I still had issues, so I gave her to my cousin. My kids were sad, and I was too. But every time I looked at her, she would remind me of my pain. That didn't last long. My cousin kept her for a season; then, Chloe came back home.

I never really got attached or close with her, so as time went on I didn't give her a break. I was hard on her. I never bonded with her, nor did I ever press the issue of her dad having a relationship with her. I really didn't need to look in his face to remind me of the weak, lustful adulteress that I was. I would ignore people and myself when we knew that it wasn't so much about me, but my daughter had more to lose than I did. I had my dad in my life; she didn't. Even though he was a grown man and he could have come, looked and called, I could have done so much more. At that point, it was not about me but her.

Many years later, I was invited to a *Raising Righteous Seed Conference.* I was there for two or three days, and I had never experienced nothing like it to this day. We have and go to all these mega conferences, but what about a parents' conference? What about your seeds? That's who Satan is after.

When I left the conference, I was driving down Manchester Ave, and everything I had ever done to hurt Chloe flashed before me. I began to cry, pray, and ask God to forgive me. He said to go to my daughter and tell her I was sorry. I cried so much to where I had to pull over. I went straight to my baby and cried out to her. I repented to her and begged her to forgive me. She acted as if everything was fine. At the time, she was about ten years old.

Then there came a time of reconciliation, bonding, changing and mending, but it wasn't easy because she was a product of all the hurt, pain, rejection, etc. When she was about twelve, she got involved in a family scandal. I went to her and let her know how much I was there for her, how much I loved and cared for her, and that I was sorry for not being there to protect her.

Now, she's growing to be a young lady. She's fifteen and thinks she has arrived. She acts like her age is backwards. Yes, fifty-one. She is so hard, rebellious, and lazy. She got to the point when I asked her to help me out at the salon she had an attitude. I said something to her, and it hurt her feelings. She hunched her shoulders at me and said, "So what." I grabbed her and took her in the restroom and disciplined her.

She didn't like it at all, but she was still walking around the shop like she was bad. She didn't want to listen, so I grabbed her hair, and I said some things that I should not have said. I found out my baby was trying and thinking of committing suicide, and it wasn't her first time thinking about doing this.

I never really thought that she would consider doing something to that degree. She feels like I never loved or wanted her, but that is not true. I've tried so much to talk and build a relationship with her, but that wasn't good enough. I run my own business, I'm in full time ministry, and I have ten grand kids. But none of it matters if I would have lost my baby to suicide, to the devil. He is a deceiver. The bible says that charity starts at home. I am to minister to my family first. Yes, I know they're the hardest ones. You know why? They know your good, bad, and ugly. But, if you can convince them that you've changed, and they become converted, then you expand your horizon within the church and out into the highways and byways. I'm sharing this because for one my life is an open book, and there are so many moms and dads that are so consumed with their jobs or ministry, and their children are falling by the wayside. Jesus said suffer not for the children to come unto Him, but how can they come to Him when we're right in the way with our issues and our day-to-day living.

They look at us and say, "If this is what it is like to be saved, I don't want it." The way they think about us and look at us is despicable. The way we live before them and the way we treat them makes them not want God. Another thing is that we want our kids to be saved and have a relationship with God, but when we get them upset or treat them wrong, they hold a lot of the stuff that we do to them against God.

Chapter Nine

Church Hurt:

Fighting for Victory!!!

Looking back to the time when I first got saved in 1992, I walked into my childhood family church, and God didn't take no time heal, deliver, and raise me up. I went to bible study and Sunday school. I don't remember them having no extra classes for leadership, but I know you had to be faithful and know your word. And we did plenty of tarrying for the Holy Ghost. I remember one week when I was tarrying, nothing happened, so I went home. But I really wanted to get filled so bad.

That night, Benny Hinn came on the T.V. I was really interested. It got to the part when he began to speak and minster through the T.V. He said he was talking to someone that was watching from home. I just knew he was talking to me. So, he began to pray for those that wanted to be filled with the Holy Ghost, and I wanted it bad because I knew that I needed it at that time. I was taught it was pretty much a must, that He is a keeper, a reminder, a guider and so much more. I knew that I needed so much more.

As he was praying, he began to touch some soft spots in my life, some areas that I had been dealing with, some pain in my body, some things that I was trying to take on the other side with me but they couldn't go because the bible says to be transformed by the renewing of your mind and to become a new creature in Christ Jesus. Then Benny Hinn said, "Somebody is at their home right now, and the Lord is dealing with you. I want you to get up from where you are and go to the television and extend your hand and touch the TV. As I extend my hand and touch and agree with you in the spirit you will be healed, delivered and set free and filled with the Holy Ghost with the evidence of speaking in tongues." I was drawn to the TV, and I put my hands on it. I began to feel a real warm feeling going through my hand and then through my body. I began to pray and cry. I started speaking in my heavenly language.

Later, he sent me his book. I believe it was free and called *Good Morning, Holy Spirit.* I believe that was the beginning of a great calling on my life. I believe that Benny Hinn had imparted something in me through the Holy Spirit that night, even for such a time as this. I've always known that I would be a great leader because as I look back to when I was in school, even in the neighborhood, people would follow me, and I would speak for them in various situations and give them advice. The advice was good and bad, but mostly good.

Every great leader has to first be a great follower, full of humility and have a spirit of servitude. Moses denounced his throne and became a slave. Then, a great leader Joshua followed and served Moses and followed the strategic plan of our great father and was able to lead the children of Israel into the Promise Land. David was a shepherd boy and a great warrior. He became a great king. Elisha served and followed Elijah until Elijah took his last breath. Elisha, then, received a double portion. Joseph had a dream and was thrown into a pit and was almost executed by his own brothers; he made it out of the pit, but he was sold and later put in jail. He went through all of that to make it to his destiny.

God didn't show Joseph all the pain, betrayal, and rejection that he would have to endure to get to the throne. It took about seventeen years for Joseph to reach his point of destiny. It also took Jesus about seventeen years to reach His purpose and destiny, after his parents found him in the temple listening to the teachers and asking questions, shocking everyone with his knowledge. Know that it is the enemy's job to hinder you and try to kill you before you reach your destiny. We all have a God-given purpose. That is the reason you were created. Your destiny is a place you were predestined to reach even before you were in your mother's womb. It was you and your Father in the spirit. You said I'll go; you can trust me, my Lord; I will complete that which you have entrusted me with.

I speak encouragement to your spirit. I speak life and life more abundantly. You shall not die but live and declare the works of the Lord. You will not die prematurely, but you shall live out all the days of your life that God has ordained and promised, in Jesus' name. I know that this journey won't be easy, but it will be worth it. You have to go through it to get to it, for the race is not given to the strong nor to the swift but to those that endure to the very end.

Paul said, "I press toward the mark of the prize of the high calling." It's a high calling, so come up in your spirit. Don't allow your present situations or your former situations to predict your future or your destiny. Have a this-too-shall-pass attitude when you get attacked or when your brothers and sisters scandalize your name. Stand on that rock which has the greatest name: Jesus. Know that all power is in His name. When the very person you're standing in the gap for seems like he/she is coming against you, don't give up. Fight even harder because the assignment didn't come from him/her but from God.

It's not about you, but it's about God's plan being carried out at any cost. For He sent His only begotten son to perish for us all so our sins may be forgiven and washed only with His blood. Only His blood was pure enough and strong enough to get the job done. Did we deserve it? Of course not, but thank Him for being a sovereign God, a merciful God, a God that's full of grace. So never forget that your life is not your life. It's been bought with a price. That price was our savior's life. That's a great price, a high price, a price that money can't pay because He paid way back on Mount Calvary.

Do yourself a favor. The next time you feel like you can't take no more and that you've had just about enough, think about Jesus just before he was betrayed by one of His own and right before He went to the Cross. He prayed to His Father and asked Him if this cup could pass, but He said nevertheless. I speak to your spirit man that you shall have a nevertheless in your spirit. It's not about you, but about who you need to minister to.

God has something on the inside of you that needs to come out for such a time as this. Be ye steadfast, unmovable, and always abounding in the word of God. Remain focused and confident in who you are and whose you are. You are victorious in Christ Jesus. You have been appointed and anointed. All you have to do is stay in your lane and be confident in who you are and what you are called to do. Don't be moved even if man tries to move you out of your position. As long as you know that God sent you there, be obedient to those that are over you and step down or aside and know that it is only temporary. There is probably more humbling that needs to take place, and a little more humility won't hurt nobody but it could help a lot of some bodies, Amen.

Know that all things work together for the good to those that love God and are called according to His purpose. Know that you are bought with a price. Your life is no longer your life. So as long as God gets the glory out of your life, you are in the right place because at the end of the day it's not about you anyway. Make sure you complete the assignment that God designed for you, no matter how long it takes to get it done, even if your flesh doesn't appreciate it and you are pretty fed up with getting the short end of the stick. You just have to realize that God created the stick, and you can use that very stick as Moses did when he took the rod and God parted the Red Sea. You can do the same thing. God does not have respect of persons.

You can take your short end of the stick and stretch it out over what is hindering you and blocking you and allow God to move everything that's blocking you. If it is hard situations, if it's intimidation, if it's jealousy, back biting, scandalizing your name, if it's something to bring you to open shame, know that these things are meant to be used as a vehicle to take you to your destiny. If it's someone that's in your life that always seems to ride you extra hard, humble yourself and pray to your Father to give you the strength that it's going to take to make it through it. You are more than a conqueror, and remember that greater is He that is in you than He that is in this world. Know that what you're going through is exactly what someone who crosses your very path is going through, and you will be able to minister to them from your heart.

As I look back for a second, and only a quick second, I was in a high place in my life. I had just got blessed with my own business, and a little while later after being faithful in the ministry, one of the ministers pulled me to the side and told me that she saw me walking very close to my pastor and so much more. She said, "Don't say anything. Let's just wait on the Lord." I said, "Amen." When I first came to the ministry, I had great concern and love and connection to the woman of God, who is my apostle now. So, I knew it was something, but I didn't know what at that time.

As time went on, after about eight months of being in the ministry, one day in the middle of service, my other pastor called me to the pulpit and said that he means no disrespect and he is not trying to take anything from me. He began to tell me about a great woman of God that goes all around the world preaching the gospel on TV and everywhere. This particular preacher had become really ill to where she could not go and minister at a certain event, so she sent her armor bearer instead. She ministered under a powerful anointing. After telling me the story, he said the Lord showed him that I was his wife's armor bearer. Then he responded, "Don't say anything. Wait on God to reveal it even more."

A couple of months later, I had been there about a year. My pastor called me over to her home one day. I just knew I was in trouble because I was known for getting rebuked and spiritually disciplined. I arrived at my pastor's house, and she called me into her office and began to minister to me. I was not expecting the words that came out her mouth. She said, "I really have been struggling with this situation, but I have to be obedient unto the Lord. I believe in this season God has called you to be my armor bearer." I knew it was from God as it had already come from three or four different ministers at different times, not including me. So, I accepted the position.

She announced it, and then it really got hot to where all hell was about to break loose. But, it wasn't like I was too accepted to begin with. I had a bold spirit, and I walked in authority, well for at least the first year. As my pastor's armor bearer, I had to aid her, pray and fast for her, and guard her. Wherever she went in the ministry, I went. God showed me a glimpse of the ministry in the future, a mega ministry. But when He sent me there, there were pretty much only family members to make up the congregation and a few close friends. That made it even harder, not to mention that my pastor was expecting someone else to be her armor bearer, but God has His reasons for the decisions that He makes.

As time went on, I was catching it from every side and not to mention correction that I had to get from my pastor. Can you believe I just knew I was full of humility, but I had a long way to go. I had to apologize when I knew for a fact I wasn't wrong. For two years, I never raised my voice, and no, I didn't curse nobody out. So I continued to stand. Having done all, I stood. I had so many plans and so much purpose in me. Not only did I not have a love and concern for the pastors, but for my Christian siblings. My pastors appointed me and anointed me with oil because God had already anointed me to be over the evangelists and to start an evangelist ministry.

Boy oh boy. They did not want to accept me even though I was good for some of them. It was like pulling their teeth without no anesthesia. Some had the spirit of sabotage, intimidation, back biting, and lying. No support made it very hard on me, but I never lost my hope or faith in God. I knew that it wasn't about me, but it was about Him and them. So, I stood, and I continued to be humble in the midst of everything.

So God blessed me with the salon, and I was the pastor's armor bearer and the head evangelist. I wasn't liked at all. And, my discernment never stopped working. You know when a sister or brother comes up, gives a hug and says I love you, but his/her actions say differently. Love is an action word. There were times when they wouldn't show any type of respect, no compassion, or no love. These are all action words. We know that love covers a multitude of sin.

When you would normally go off on someone, you apply love and compassion instead of snapping someone's head off or stabbing someone in the heart with your hurtful words. It's really time to be quick to hear, slow to speak and slow to anger. Those are signs of maturity. I always did well in that area. I would simply treat people the way I desired to be treated, even to the point when certain people would be all up in my face yelling and using hand movements. I haven't always been saved and sanctified, but I charged it to God and not to their hearts. I took it that the Lord had some more humbling to work out in me. As time went on, about a year later came some great humility.

On a Friday afternoon, I was in my salon *Anointed Touch* when Gerry, a stranger, walked in. After we exchanged greetings, we immediately felt a connection. Eventually, we began dating. Approximately three weeks later, I invited Gerry to be my guest at church. Gerry agreed and began to attend church services with me on a regular basis. Six months into the relationship, we began marriage counseling.

After three months of marriage counseling, I told Gerry I thought it would be best if we both spent some time alone with God and not with each other. My intent was for both of us to go into our secret and quiet places to fellowship with the Lord. Gerry did not like my idea one bit.

He told me that he was not in agreement with my idea and that he wanted to move forward with the relationship at that point rather than take the suggested break. Because I had a made-up mind to seek and hear from God, I did not push the issue when Gerry decided to end the relationship and walk away.

Not a month later, another young lady, Felicia, came to the church. After some time passed, Gerry and Felicia began dating. Felicia learned of Gerry and my relationship, and she began to taunt me by sitting next to me and making remarks about how I let my Boaz get away. Two months later, Gerry and Felicia were married. However, it was not a marriage that would last.

After six months of dreadful matrimony, Gerry and Felicia separated. During the time of the marriage and afterwards, I had many opportunities to minister to Felicia, and I did just that. Through my own hurt and pain of the broken relationship with Gerry, I stood with the strength God poured into me.

In return for receiving God's healing virtue, I poured healing and strength into Felicia, who then too was suffering from a broken relationship: a failed marriage. I could have turned a blind eye or a deaf ear to Felicia, but instead, I put my hurt, disappointment and pride aside to see to the need of my sister in Christ. Through my love and obedience to God, I was able to minister to Felicia and show her sisterly love as well as show brotherly love to Gerry. As time went on, Felicia and I developed a friendship. Now, we can lean on each other in our times of need.

Chapter Ten

Don't Stop Dreaming

One day, I was sitting in my living room in the cool of the day. I had a hangover from the night before. I was in a backslidden condition. As I sat on the couch, I dozed off. At least I thought I dozed off, but it was God that came to me in a vision. I had entered into a large stadium that I had never seen or been to before. I entered in at the right side of the stage, and I was wearing all white. I began to check the lights and sound system. I looked over to my far left and saw people coming in two and three hours early, and I said, "Wow. They're here to get the best seats. They're the early birds for real." This stadium had mega thousands of seats.

I sat up on the couch, and I spoke to God and said, "Whatever I have to do to get to that point, I willing, I knew that was a beginning point of my destiny. He showed me a glimpse of my destiny, and I liked what I saw at that point in my life. I had already been running from my purpose and the calling that was on my life. I ran all the way from South Central L.A. to Rialto, CA. I knew that I had a great calling on my life and that I was chosen by God. But, I allowed fear and intimidation to grip me. I would mess up, run off, or back slide, but when God showed me a glimpse of my purpose and destiny, instead of running from it, I began to run towards it. God is so amazing.

In that very hour, I began to get up off the couch. My cousin was living with me, and you know how it is when two women live in the same house. Plus, she was on some extra stuff, so we were actually walking around in my house and not speaking. But on this particular day, I was walking towards the kitchen from the living room, and she was walking from the hall. We met up, and she cleared her throat and said to me, "You know, I need to tell you something." If she could have held it, she would have. But, she didn't have a choice. She had to release it or maybe she thought I wouldn't have received it from her from the way she had been acting while staying at my house. Anyway, she said, "You know, God deals with me in dreams, and I just dreamed that you were on a big platform a stage. You had the same anointing that was on Benny Hinn. You were so anointed and on fire for God. All you would do was wave your hands or blow, and the people would fall out and be healed." She said, "You had a team of people that were behind you, and I was one of them."

Within that same week, I remember I would ask my girls to help me to stop drinking alcohol. At the time, I was drinking every day.

Every time they would try to help me, I would go off on them or make up a sad excuse. Right when I was so tired, after my vision on the couch, I was drinking a beer. As I was coming out of the kitchen, my son, who was ten years old at the time, was coming down the hallway. As he approached me, he said, "Mama if you don't stop drinking that stuff, you're going to die and go to hell." I stopped. I didn't know whether to knock his head off or what, but I knew it was GOD. It could have only been him. My hand started to shake and my legs started to move towards the kitchen. All I could do was pour the beer down the sink. I haven't drunk any liquor since. Boy oh boy. What can come out of a babe's mouth? To God be the Glory.

I am sharing this with you to let you know don't stop dreaming. My first dream was in 2000, and it's twelve years later. Joseph had a dream, and he didn't reach it until seventeen years and a whole lot of trials, tests, and suffering later. So, don't stop dreaming and don't give up on your dream. It's the key to your destiny.

I knew I would need a covering, more training and deliverance. My kids had been inviting me to the little church by the liquor store. I wouldn't ever go because I was fed up with church people, not God, but His people. But, at that point, I went to visit, and I liked what I saw and felt. So, I went again and again and again. Eventually, I joined. From there, I went to the new members' class, and then the leadership class, and then to an intense class that our bishop taught for a six-week course. You had to have already finished the leadership class to take the course. In this class, you could not be late, and you could not miss.

It was a class that would show your accountability, integrity, reliability and dependability. I completed it, and then I went through the S.H.A.P.E. class that his son Pastor Carlos Martin diligently taught; it was awesome.

My life has never been the same. I'm actually writing a book from that class dealing with the mind, body, and soul- the complete man. I was under their ministry for at least eight years. Then, about five years later, after my vision on the couch, I got a call. They said my mom was in the hospital and that she was in a coma. She was diagnosed with Lung Cancer, and they gave her five days to live. All the church I had been going to, the classes and getting closer to God wasn't enough. He wanted more. He wanted all. He wanted all of me. He wanted my life for His life, for my mother's life. As a matter of fact, I had backslid again and had started back drinking. Yes, after all that; it happens to the best.

So, I got on the freeway and began to pray. I had never prayed like I did that day. I started out by thanking Him for everything He had ever done for my family and me. I even thanked Him for the things He didn't do, and then I repented to Him for all of my wrong doings, my sins, transgressions, and iniquities too. I told Him I was so sorry and asked if He would find it in His heart to please forgive me. Then, I petitioned Him on behalf of my mother. You see, some people received Christ at a revival and some by going to church with a loved one or some on their sick or deathbed, but I was united with Christ through a bargain. I told God, "If you save my mom, if you bring her out of this, I will serve you for the rest of my life. I will never turn my back on you, Lord if you save her." I pleaded for my mother's life. You see, you could call me the backslidden queen before my mom got sick. I had backslid three times over a period of eight years.

I made it to the hospital, and my mom did not look like my mom. I barely recognized her. It hurt me to my heart because it had been a while since I had seen my mom. I was still a run-away child as an adult, sad to say. So, we were all at the hospital. My mom was in a coma. They said they overdosed her, so we prayed.

Later, we walked outside into the parking lot. They were all calling my name: my uncle, my brother, and close friends. Many of them that were there are not alive today. They were asking who was getting the liquor, what are we drinking, and what store we were going to meet at. I simply said, "Now is not the time for drinking." A couple of seconds later, a man called me by my name and said, "Katrina, come here." I did, and he said that God has need of me, there is greatness in me, and I am going to draw plenty of people to Christ. Then He said, "Your loved one that's on their deathbed is not going to die. It's through you that they are spared, but God wants all of you this day and for the rest of your life. At this same time tomorrow, your loved one is going to get up out of their deathbed."

God's power and presence was all around my car. I began to cry out. I repented again, and I purged right outside in the parking lot. The man said, "I'm not going to touch you. I want you to feel the power of God without my touch." That's exactly what happened, and my little mean sister who doesn't know much at all about God felt the presence of God too. The guy went over to her window and asked her, "You feel something don't you that you've never felt before?" She was crying and scared, but he asked her if she wanted to know and get closer to God. She said yes, and he told her to stick close to me, but she didn't and she has great regrets from that. I'll talk to you a little later on about that.

I stayed at the hospital day and night. I didn't even go home to take a bath. I felt like if they gave her five days to live, I was going to spend all those days there with her. The next day, my uncle told my sister and me to go to his house and take a bath and nap. He said he would watch our mom for us. So, we left and went to take our baths and lay across his bed to rest. A little time went by and the phone rung. It was my uncle. He said, "If you'll girls don't come and get your mama. She is up here, done got up, and trying to walk to the restroom and was about to fall on my watch talking about she got to pee with a catheter in her." We started praising God. My sister said, "Wait a minute. What time is it?" It was a little past the time that the man who prayed for me had said she would get up, not wake up, but get up. I believe after going to several churches in L.A., I knew I was entertaining an angel. To this day, I have never turned away from God. It has been He and I all the way. Thank you, my Lord.

My mom came out of the hospital and battled Cancer and other health problems, but I was there with her every step of the way. When she was a little better, I moved them to Rialto with me. They got an apartment in my building, but she was still sick. She would struggle to breathe and would be on life support and oxygen. There was a time when I was sitting still enough because I had taken off work to take care of my mom. I sat there looking at my mom, and it just hit me like a ton of bricks. Suddenly, I said in my mind *you can't die. I have too many things that I have not told you.* I took out my notebook from my bible bag and began to write.

It's amazing how God has been downloading certain things into my spirit, even the day before I go to church. I know the very thing that my pastor is going to preach or someone else will come and minister and boom- there it is- another word of confirmation.

I knew that God was talking to me like crazy in this season of my life. One thing I do know is He is going to use me like crazy. I know it's big. I just have to continue to pray for humility because it is not an easy task to stay humble even when the Lord has exalted you. That's the very thing that caused Satan to be thrown out of heaven: a proud and puffed spirit. You know, he had a very high place or shall I say position in heaven. He was praise and worship and very beautiful. Then, he lost all access to heaven, eternal life, beauty and praise. Do you think he's not pissed off with us? He actually wants to kill, steal and destroy us because we have dominion, authority and are joint heirs with Christ. We have access to eternal life.

Just remember, Satan is going to try everything he can to get you off your course that God has set before you. You must be strong and courageous. Know that even when you fall or slip or slide a little, as long as you hold on to your savior and don't let him go, you will be okay. Just see yourself in the boxing ring. It's you and the devil. He has knocked you down with a hard under the belt blow, and the hit was so devastating that you actually almost went out. But, you didn't. You grabbed whatever substance that's in you, and the main substance is Jesus. You began to call on the name of Jesus like you lost your mind because there is so much power in His name. There is all power in His name. You must begin to put the word of God on the devil, and he, his demons and imps must go. When you begin to get up and get back in the fight, the devil will try to remind you of your past. Just remind him of his future. Know that all things work together for the good to those who love God and are called according His purpose.

As I have run this race and have fought this battle, I've found out that I'm actually in a battle with myself, yes me against me. It is my flesh warring against my spirit. There is no good thing in my flesh. It's hostile and dominating. It wants to be the stronger vessel, but not so. You have to be like Paul when he said he beat his flesh. You have to put the flesh under subjection. It has to die daily, or it will rule the body. So, you put the flesh under subjection by not giving it what it wants when it wants but what it needs. For instance, fasting and praying. Your flesh don't want to do it, but your spirit needs to do it to survive. So, you must begin fasting and praying consistently. Both the spirit and the body need to eat to survive, so whichever one you feed the most will be the strongest. And, the one that you feed the most is the one that rules the most.

So, even in the midst of a storm, trial or tribulation, if you continue to trust and obey God and praise and worship Him in all that you do, your spirit man will be built up. That will make him stronger. On the other hand, a lot of us want to feed our flesh. When the Lord wakes me around four and five in the morning, my spirit tells me to get up, but my body tells me no. Whichever one we find ourselves giving into, that's the strongest. When you find yourself with other folks' business on your tongue more than your own business, the flesh is ruling. When your spirit is telling you that you're talking too much, talk less and listen more, or better yet, don't talk at all until God says so. It's hard I know, but greater is He that is in you than he that's in this world. Or, is the he that's in this world in you too?

One night while I was asleep, the Lord visited me in my dream. All I could remember was that I was at a place where I was going down a walkway, and I saw crowds of people on both sides. I was walking, and there was a team of people around me. The crowd of people was yelling, "Can I have your autograph? Can I have your autograph?" They were reaching out to touch my hands. I was reaching out to them as well, but my people that were with me kept pushing me forward and telling me to keep moving forward. But, I felt like Jesus at that point in my dream when He rebuked His disciples and told them to suffer not the children to come unto Him. I felt so close and connected with the people. I was full of God's compassion.

My dream felt so real that when I began to wake up and come into this earthly realm, my hand was extended out as if I were touching the people right in the room where I was. It was amazing. When I woke up, I said to the Lord, "What was that, my Lord?" All he told me at that point was to start writing. I didn't question Him or talk back out loud, but I said, "Yea right, with my busy schedule, with raising my kids and grandkids, and running my own business, and in full-time ministry. Now you want me to make time to write?" There was a willingness in my spirit. I wanted that dream to come to pass.

My son normally slept with me, but this particular night I fell asleep in my daughter's bed downstairs. Shortly after I woke up, my son came down the stairs and said, "Mama, I had a dream or a vision, and I saw you on the Oprah Winfrey Show. You had on a certain color, and she had a book in one hand and was holding your hand in her other hand presenting you to her audience."

Oh, it is time for self examination. You always want to do a self examination to see what is going on in you, so you will know where you are even when others may see something going on in you. You will know or you won't be that far off. That goes for our physical bodies as well. It's healthy for the mind, body, and soul. Get my upcoming book *Shape Up or Ship Out* for a deeper revelation. It's imperative for us to do regular checkups. Neglecting to do so gives the enemy a step ahead of you because in dealing with the spiritual examination, you don't want be so easily deceived.

Check your prayer life. Make sure you're living a fasted life. Make sure you spend intimate time with your maker. Are you eating God's Word on a daily basis? Do you find yourself telling little white lies? That's what some people call them, but anything other than the truth is a lie. Are you full of compromise, halfway full of it, or do you just compromise for emergencies only? How is your heartbeat? Is it beating only for God and the things of God? Or, do you find yourself having an irregular heartbeat for the things of this world? With all due respect, that skipped beat is Satan in the mix. You got to get him all the way out. He gets nothing.

The bible says that above all the heart of man is wicked. It also says that wherever our money is, there is our heart. The bible also says that the issues of life flow through the heart. God said that He searches our hearts. That's how He knows everything about us. So, make sure your heart is pure and cleansed. If it needs to be cleansed, He can clean it. He is known to be the finest of all, dealing with the heart. He is the heart specialist, a heart regulator. If it's in really bad shape and if He sees it necessary, He will give you a new heart. Yes, a heart transplant. I've known Him to do it. But, you have to make sure your body won't reject it with all the mess that it's been through, misused and abused too.

Dealing with the natural heart, if you have a bad heart and you are even able to get on the transplant list, there are certain criteria that you have to meet. You first have to lose weight. On the spiritual side, the weight is sin that you need to lose. Another requirement is that you have to eat differently. You can no longer eat the old foods you used to eat that got you in the predicament you're in. On the spiritual side, instead of eating so much physical food, you have more of an appetite for spiritual food and for fasting and praying. Praise and worship is your spiritual exercise. Some people have a heart transplant, and their body just rejects it. I believe that when God gives you a clean and new heart, you have to work at it to maintain a healthy heart. Don't allow your old traits to rise up or come in and clog up your arteries with gossip, back biting, anger and a lot more, just to name a few. You know where you're falling short. Don't even entertain the thoughts. As soon as they come up, cast them down immediately.

How is your blood flow? Have you been so hurt and misused and abused to where there has been so much damage done from people and yourself to where your arteries are all clogged up and your blood vessels are busted and weak? You need them to be repaired, and some need to be replaced. Some people can get their arteries unclogged meaning they allow God to go in and clean out everything that's not of Him, even the little things that they barely want to acknowledge as sin.

The one thing that you seem to be unable to shake is the very thing that is connected to other things. Whatever causes a separation between you and your Father has to be cleaned out and eliminated because it can be that very thing that causes you to not make it in through the pearly gates. Don't be deceived. That's one of Satan's greatest weapons. Just know that your whole life here reflects on when you leave here. Yes, we need to make sure we walk in and carry out our purpose and destiny. At the end of your destiny is judgment. Make sure your heart is pure. Make sure you're connected with your Father. Make sure He's able to say (put your name right here) ___________, thy good and faithful servant, a job well done. You may enter in. That's your main purpose on this earth. What would it profit a man to gain the whole world and lose his soul? When you find yourself holding on and standing, continue to stand and hold on. It's how you hold on in grace, knowing after being tried by the fire that you will come forth as pure gold, pure enough to be used like never before.

I know that there is so much more that my Father has for me to do in a higher dimension, which leads me to tell you of one particular night. After coming out of praise and worship, I had my newest edition to my family: my ninth grandchild Breille. She sat there like she was in the spirit as well; her look said *can you change me now, please*. So. I took her to the restroom, and I looked in the mirror. I began to think *the way I'm feeling right now, I need this more often.* When I'm in worship with God, when I'm in His presence, I feel so strong, like I can conquer anything. I feel like I can leap mountains. There's no stress, worries, burdens, bills, sickness, or pain. So, there I was standing in the restroom in my church on a Wednesday evening at bible study. I said, "How can I feel like this more often because when I leave church, and sometimes I don't even get to leave yet, I'm disturbed in my spirit?" When I go home, there are issues with kids. I'm thinking and stressing sometimes in the car before I even make it home or to work.

You know, just to back it up for a second, throughout my life and my Christian walk, I often wondered how everything would feel so good and right when I was at church on Sunday and Wednesday but the rest of the week would be stressful and a hot mess. I would be robbing Peter to pay Paul, ducking and dodging people and bill collectors, lying and all kinds of stuff. I had reached the point where I was tired of it. I needed so much more than that. I knew that God was not pleased with me. God requires us to live a holy, sanctified life. He said don't worry for tomorrow for tomorrow has enough problems itself. He said if He provides for the lilies in the field and for the birds, and if He sent His only begotten Son to lay His life down, what would He withhold from you. He said to cast all your burdens on Him for He cares for you. He said His yoke is easy and His burdens are light. He said he will withhold no good thing from you. He said He will take off the spirit of heaviness and put on a garment of praise. He will give you beauty for ashes and turn your tears of sorrow to tears of joy. That's the kind of God we serve.

Back to what God had told me. He said I had lived a life of worship. Worship Him in everything I do. Stay in Him. I remember people saying you can't always be in the spirit, but I beg to differ. He said, "Always abide in me, and I'll abide in you." So, what I'm saying is, if we spend more time communing with God, we would be so much better off. Every day we should worship Him, giving Him the reverence that He deserves.

Can you honestly say, knowing God is looking down at you right now, that you give God all the glory that is due to Him seven days a week and that you worship Him in your giving and your living, the way you talk to people, and the way you spend your money? For real, you know it's God's money. He just trusts you with the ninety percent just to see what you do with it. So, do you lie to the bill collectors? Do you have an income that you know you shouldn't be getting? Are you on housing plus working and getting child support and only reporting what you want to report? Well, I've got news to tell you. All you're doing is holding up your own blessings. It's like getting money and putting it in a paper bag with a hole in it.

Trust God with the little, and watch Him blow on it and make it more than enough. You will have all the peace you need right there. Trust God over every area of your life. Stop picking and choosing what you want Him to handle. I dare you to give it all to Him. Yea, I know it's much easier saying than doing, but believe me if I had got this deliverance earlier, I would have been on my twelfth book. This one would have been written and released eight years ago, but God knows I got some catching up to do. I got to catch up to my destiny. So, what I'm trying to say is worship Him in all that you do. The same way you praise and worship Him at church, do it at home, in your car, at a friend's house and in your decisions. See, most people won't lie in God's house. You should give Him that same reverence in your house and everywhere you go because really you are the sanctuary. So, wherever you find yourself, let God be glorified and your enemy be scattered. We were created to worship Him, but we find so little time to give Him what is due.

The same night, a few hours later, I had been up all night. I don't know what happened, but I just fell again and gave into this filthy flesh. I believe there are spirits still lingering in my house. I hated being a slave to my flesh, to sin, to a perverted spirit. I hated it, and I felt so bad. I didn't feel worthy at all. I was so sorry. I repented, and I asked God to forgive me.

I said, "You know me. You know what I've been though, and you know the things that I'm going to do before I even do it. I need help. I need you to take this thing from me. I ask for complete healing. I need complete transformation. I need a renewed life. Deliver me, Lord please, so that I won't continue to allow the enemy to win over my spirit. I did a horrible thing in your sight. I just disregarded you. Will you ever forgive and cleanse me from all unrighteousness? I denounce you, Satan in the name of Jesus Christ. The demons and imps too. I am no longer your slave. You no longer rule over my life. My life belongs to Jesus. He paid a high price for my life, and the price was His life. I am so sorry, Jesus for defiling my temple, a place where the Holy Spirit should reside, but now I am unclean. Though my sins be as red as crimson, you said come and let us reason together that you will wash me with hyssop, and I will be whiter than snow. I break and pull up every generational curse that was assigned to my family's bloodline. I ask for forgiveness for my ancestors, for any voodoo, witchcraft, every satanic ritual, and every vow commitment that was spoken out of their mouths. Please forgive them, and I ask you to sever all soul ties. Lord, I need help. You delivered me from Crack Cocaine. You delivered me from being an alcoholic. You delivered me from being a whoremonger and so much more. Heal me from myself. It's my mind. I need help with this thing. It has been with me since I was a child. When I was a child, I thought as a child and acted as a child. But when I grew up, I put away childish things. I ask you again this time to forgive me and throw it in the sea of forgetfulness and allow me at the appointed time to forgive myself. For I know that the weapons of warfare are not carnal but mighty to the pulling down of strongholds, bringing into captivity every vain imagination, every unclean thought, every foul spirit. I dislodge every imp and demon and curse, every negative word, every word that was spoken is canceled, every word that has been spoken over my life that is contrary to the word of God that my Father which art in heaven has declared over my life and my children's lives and my grandchildren's lives and down how ever far through my bloodline that this declaration can go. It shall come to pass in Jesus' name."

One Sunday night after church, my grandchildren and I were lying in my bed and little Katrina said she wanted to feel God and cry to Him like I did. So, I began to minister to all my grandchildren, to where they could understand, about how the Holy Spirit works, I told them that God is someone and to speak out to Him. The Holy Spirit will carry it out. As I would explain it, the five year old would finish my sentences. I knew at that point, she was ready. So, I began to pray, and she started to cry and say Jesus for about twenty minutes. I saw I was scaring her, and I was a little moved as well because I had never seen nothing like that before out of my twenty years of being saved. After she stopped crying, she said, "Let me pray for you." She prayed for me; then, she told her mom, who never goes to church and who has some issues, "Mama, raise your hand. Raise your hands. I'm gone pray for you."

Her mom scooted her hands right up being obedient to the authority that her daughter was operating in and boldness like never before. My granddaughter began to pray, intercede and prophesy. She began to say, "You will get in a car and you will have an accident, crash and die." She kept on praying, but I was already tired. I said, "I know she has an apostolic anointing on her life." She kept going and going, so I counter prayed against death, and we went to sleep.

My daughter called me about an hour later and asked me if I had heard about my little cousin. I asked, "What happened?" She said she heard one of our cousins say that our cousin had had an accident and didn't make it. When I found out the time it happened, it was at the same time my granddaughter was praying. What happened was really weird to the point where I don't take it lightly that my granddaughter was praying in my bed about the very thing to the bull's eye. I know there is a significant reason in this.

To be of assistance to my family, I took my grown self out to the desert to support my cousin. When I got there, there was so much going on. First of all, let me back up. I didn't even have my own car at the time. Anytime I had ever gone around my family, especially my dad, I had to have my own vehicle because at any given time I most likely had to bounce for real. So, they came and picked me up. That was a big no-no. That was the first warning sign that I chose to ignore. So, I was out there and my cousins and some of my sisters and brothers were there as well. Most of them were tuned-up, as they say it, full of liquor and whatever else. I had never been around so many cigarettes since before I was saved.

They were in a trance from a certain song. As they would dance, they would get real loud and start play fighting, but I thought it was a real fight. It made me very uncomfortable, so after awhile, I went upstairs and went in the house. I wasn't up there too long when my little cousin bust in the door. She went to the kitchen drawer and grabbed a knife. I jumped up and grabbed her. My sister and her mom grabbed her too; all three of us were struggling with her trying to get the knife from her without getting hurt or hurting her. All I could see in the spirit was her ramming that knife right in my stomach, but she couldn't. I was blocked. I knew that because as her mom and my sister were trying to get the knife from her, she was biting them. She did not attempt to hit or bite me. We got the knife from her, and we took her into her mom's room.

As she sat on the floor, I really began to pray. I saw that she was possessed because I would hear her speak; then, the spirit showed up and spoke. So, I started to plead the blood of Jesus, and I grabbed my anointed oil. She said, "No! What's that? What you doing?" Her mom said no about the oil because of some of her religious reasons. I respected her for a minute, but once I got tired of toiling around with her and that spirit, I told the spirit to reveal itself. I asked him who he was, and she began to stick her tongue out and twirl it around and in and out. It was very vulgar and had a large ring in it.

When her mother saw that, she turned around and ran out of the room. Immediately, I grabbed the blessed oil, put it on her, and started to pray. But, before I could get deep into my prayer, she was tripping out big time. I spoke to the spirit, so it could talk back and I could call it out by name and cast it out. But, baby let me tell what really happened. You see, I went by myself and that was a big no-no. The second warning was when God said go two-by-two, but I was all alone in the natural realm. My cousin had turned Muslim, and my sister was drinking and running from her calling. So, I had put the oil on her. She wasn't moved. That spirit was so strong in her and bold to where it tapped me on my forehead as if to say I was wasting my time and it wasn't going nowhere.

Earlier, I knew that it was a bit much, and I wasn't spiritually equipped at the time. I was by myself spiritually and overdue with quadruplets, burnt out, and exhausted. And I recognized that that spirit was very strong, dominate, and bold. At that time, I was fragile, weak, and open. But, I had enough sense to look at it after it tapped me on my head. I wasn't even for it. I turned around and walked out the door. I knew that I was there really due to disobedience, so the best thing at that point was to get out of there. That was Godly wisdom.

At that point that was my cue to roll on home, but I didn't have my car. So I had to stick it out. I went to my little cousin's house and prayed and got whatever sleep I could get. The next morning, we got up and drove to LA to make the funeral arrangements. Then, they took me home at about twelve o'clock or one o'clock early the next morning.

My church was planning a leadership trip, and we were to leave that next morning at six. So, I had to go home, finish packing, and wash out a few things that I needed. But I received a call, and they said we were going to leave at one in the afternoon, so I pressed my way. I was able to pay my rent with my cousin's help. I was able to pay for the rest of my trip, and I didn't have any more money after that.

Now, the old me wouldn't have considered going thousands of miles away from home with no money. But the new and improved mature me went thousands of miles on faith because I knew not only did my very life depend on it, but several lives and my purpose and destiny awaited. I couldn't believe that I slept the whole trip there. I've never trusted anyone's driving but mine and my pastor's driving, but he was under attaché with his physical health, so he didn't drive. I only woke for food and to use it. That was crazy. It wasn't me at all. Once we got there, we got settled and dressed for the evening service.

We began with praise and worship service, and I had come expecting everything that God had for me. Signs, wonders, and miracles were released in the atmosphere, so I praised and worshiped the Lord and danced for Him like never before. I didn't want to give the flesh no room. Even though I was a little faded, I pressed and worshipped and praised radically because I had come so far. I wanted everything I had come for. They opened up in a night of praise, and that was right on time for me because God said to enter into His gates with thanksgiving and enter His courts praise. I fitted right in because I love to praise and worship the Lord. I blended right in because I always had a radical praise. It's just that over the time and fellowship, it began to go out over different situations and circumstances. My praise seemed to be kindled down. But when I got to Oklahoma, it was on and cracking. I had a radical praise, and I worshiped God the way He was due.

The next day, they had a day service, then a dinner too. There was a song that was ministering. It was a song with the words- *it's your season to give birth.* The singer said that there was someone in the house who was about to give birth. As soon as the minister began to get in a birthing position, I believe I was already beginning to hurt like

I never have. I found myself on the floor in the middle of the aisle. I had a midwife that was there praying with me, but I felt a pain in my lower back that I never felt while having a natural baby. Then the service was over.

Later that night, we went to the dinner. I sat there in pain, and the apostle of the house said my water had broken. My pastor didn't even know at that point what I was going through. Even when the preacher was preaching, I was travailing. I went to the restroom, and I was in major pain. Someone heard me and asked me if I was ok. I don't remember what I replied. I came out of the stall, and she said that I was in labor. At first, she began to pray for me, but I knew I had to get out of the restroom because I wasn't with that bathroom ministering, especially because I didn't know the lady. She sat me down on a purple chair under a palm tree. How amazing! I really began to get louder and louder.

At that time, my pastors and the rest had gone to the pastors' quarters. I heard the elder going to get my sister in Christ from my church. She went to get the evangelist and told her to take me out of the church. They started to walk me out. When I passed through the doorway, I heard someone from their ministry say something like some spirits couldn't stay there. Our evangelist said 'entertaining spirit,' and then I got in the van and sat down. The elder got in and began to say a foul spirit, and she began to spit up. I was in the back in pain, and I started to purge. The young girl next to me began to holler and say she saw some type of demon.

We made it to the hotel, and that's where it really went down. I got out of the van, and one of the pastors from my church was there. They began to tell him something, and he took me to my room. They treated me like an alien or the woman with the issue of blood or the man with leprosy. They were assuming from the young girl's reaction that I was possessed, so they took me to my room and left me there. The girl was acting a mess. She was possessed. They started to put blessed oil on the doors and were speaking in tongues. I never knew a demon to flee from speaking in tongues. Later on, one of my sisters came up to check on me. She said no one would come with her, so she came by herself. Maybe the pastor that walked me up came back with her.

My pastor came later and asked me to come down to her room. She asked me what happened, and I began to tell her. Towards the end of me telling what happened, the other pastor, who was the girl's pastor, began to question me and said that everybody was saying that it was me and that I was attacked by the enemy. She started to pray for me and laid hands and then poured oil down my throat twice. I was in agreement, but I was very watchful and uncomfortable with the way things had been going on. So as she was praying for me, the evangelist, who called out 'entertaining spirit' at the church and had taken me out, grabbed my throat and said something. I began to purge, and when they were asking which spirit they were dealing with, I said, "Death" out of my mouth. I don't know where it came from. I don't know if there was a point of contact or if my pastors where saying that they felt like I was possessed as well. I was healed after they prayed for me, but it was something that the pastor said while she was praying. She said that I could not give birth the way the baby was positioned. She said that it was breach, and that it would die. When she said that, the elder that was there said, "It got to die." Then, I began to pray, battle, cry out to God, saying, "Not so."

Later, the pastor told me that when she was praying my baby had turned around and was in an upright position. So, I went to my room and the sisters that had been staying with me didn't even want to stay with me anymore, and that was fine because I never felt too connected anyway. Normally, my pastors never stay on Sundays. They leave that Sunday morning at the break of dawn, but the apostle told them the night before that they needed to stay. I believe my pastor had got rebuked earlier that day, so they decided to stay. I was happy because God knew that I did not want to leave like that.

We went to the morning service, and she called an altar call. She poured oil down my throat and that made the third time: one for the Father, the Son and the Holy Ghost. I lay out on the floor as if I had been put to sleep with anesthesia. He was performing a C-section, and I didn't feel a thing. After the service, I went to the restroom. I did not want to leave like that without things being handled. Yet, did I trust God?

As I was in the restroom using it before we hit the road, someone came in and said that the apostle wanted to see me. She was standing in the hallway right next to the spot where they sat me the night before when all that stuff was going on. She asked, "What happened, baby?" I began to tell her. She asked if it felt like I was in labor. I told her yes.

Then she asked one of her prophets that was there that I didn't even know was there if they evaluated what they had heard.

They both said that they heard birthing pains, and it was not demonic activity. Then, the apostle said that they never should have taken me out of the sanctuary. She said that the devil was trying to kill and stop my destiny. The elder that was in the room when they were praying for me looked over at me and said, "Yea, you lost your baby, huh?" I said, "Oh, but no." She rebuked them and asked why they would take me out of the church. The elder from the night before who first started to purge said that she was embarrassed, and I was too loud, so she made the call to take me out.

I'm sure the devil and his demons and imps were waiting. They couldn't do nothing inside the church, but as soon as we passed the door post, I believe we were attacked. Before I went to Oklahoma, I remember someone telling me that I would give birth in a secluded place. It would not be in my regular habitation. When I was at the table, the evangelist said she saw in the spirit that I would have to hide away to give birth. When I sat back and meditated on everything, God showed me when I was first on the floor, I gave birth on that birth song. When I was at the table, I gave birth and when I left out of the restroom and sat on the purple chair under the palm tree, I gave birth. Last, but not least, out of the four, I gave birth at the altar when the oil was poured down my throat. I went out, and I didn't feel any pain, but I knew that God was performing a C-section on me. So, I gave birth to quadruplets. This book is my first book. *Born to Lead* will be my second. *Shape Up or Ship Out* will be my third one. My book of notes will be my fourth one.

When I made it home, I had a cycle. I had not had one in a year, and it was heavier than it had ever been. It lasted seven days. It's something about His blood.

I began to walk in confidence. I knew God was with me. I felt like the woman with the issue of blood after she was made whole. So as I filled in the gap of sin that separated me from God, my life seemed to get better and better. Even though it didn't seem like it in the physical, it was in the spiritual. One day, I was reunited with my old close friend that I hadn't been with in years. Somewhere down over the years, our relationship began to be seasonal. I believe the season I met up with her was a good season. I believe that was a season for iron to sharpen iron. God used each of us to tear down everything that was not of Him and to rebuild and build that which the enemy counted out.

We shall complete the good works that God has begun in us. We will go out into the highways and hedges to compel the people to come in and write about the hurt and pain from your sister. I know that God has not brought me this far to leave me now. I've come this far by faith, and I am learning how to lean on Him, trusting in His holy name, knowing that there is no name above His name, knowing that we've misused His name. We say we are children of God, ambassadors of Christ. But do we truly live the life of holiness, a life with a clean and pure heart and clean hands.

Have you or are you really willing to give up the very thing you know that's keeping you from being close and intimate with Him. Don't be fooled. God is not mocked. He looks high and low. He sees all. That's one you can't hide from. While you are steadily busy trying to hide and convince mere man that you got it all together, there God is looking right at you hoping that you will denounce the enemy and take on Christ. Stop bringing Him to an open shame over and over again. It's time out for continuing to allow the enemy to keep me quiet. He's been having my mouth shut while the people thought I was talking. But no more spirit of intimidation and fear. God has put something great in me and it's high time that it shines. Hallelujah! Amen! My spirit agrees with that. I got to give Him praise!

Chapter Eleven

From Pain to Purpose

I never thought my subtitle would cost me so much. I thought God was talking about my past pain, but oh no. He wanted me to come from a whole other place, a place of great hurt, pain and regrets. Yes, I have a few regrets concerning my dad. I know I'm not perfect, but I could have done better. When my dad had first got sick, I knew it was serious but not that serious. I didn't take the time to help him like I should have. I would do all kind of things for my mom when she was sick, but when it came to my dad, I would make suggestions. But, I wouldn't enforce or follow through with them.

One reason was because he was very head strong. He did what he wanted to do, and he didn't want to try the methods that I had because drinking alcohol just didn't mix with it. Right when my dad was ready to go through the herbal program with me and move to my house, or at least he made me think he was, it didn't happen. He died two days later. I never got a chance to take care of my dad. I used to tease him by saying, "I can't wait until you slow down, so that I can get you your rocking chair, with house shoes and you can kick back and let me take care of you." He said, "Oh no, you're not. You ain't gone get me in no rocking chair." I most certainly didn't. I used to feel like he would cut up too much. He was almost seventy years old, and he would still cut up with his kids, grandkids, and if he had to his greatgrands too.

He didn't slow down until he really began to get sick. After talking to him and other people, I realized my dad was getting closer and closer to Jesus, and that was a blessing. He used to tell me that I just don't know but he and the Man upstairs is tight. He said they were partners, and the way it looked, it seems like they were.

Shortly after, I received a call from my sister saying my dad was in the ambulance being rushed to the hospital. I knew it was serious because he never allowed anyone to place him in the ambulance nor take him to the hospital. A couple of days later, my kids and I went to visit him, and we had an awesome visit. On the seventh day, my sister called me in a frantic state and said, "Daddy isn't doing well at all." At that point, I rushed to the hospital, but by the time I arrived, he was already gone. As I sat by his bedside, the pain of his loss was unbearable. At that point, all of my strength was gone. I had to completely depend on God's strength to carry on.

Sometime after my dad passed, I was in the bath, and I hadn't been feeling God's presence around me. I hadn't been praying or fasting like I usually would, and I had not been reading my word like I should.

I was sitting there examining the things in my life for the last four months, and all I could hear was everybody else's voice so loud in my ears and spirit. I really couldn't hear my Heavenly Father's voice, so there I was sitting there feeling like I was in a dry dark desolate place. I felt like those dry bones in the book of Ezekiel. My bones felt dead and dry. I told the Lord that I had to hear His voice. If I didn't hear another person's voice, as long as I heard from Him, it was fine. "It's so crazy right now," I told Him, "all I need is one word, just one word, and I will be alright." If I'm at a place where I'm only hearing from my mentors, pastors, and friends, and I can't hear God, then Houston we have a problem.

I'm just keeping it real. Can I keep it real? I really need to because this is my life, and it is what it is. I really need to be real. Like I was saying, if I hear man's voice in my head, then that's who I'm serving. That's who has been having my most undivided attention. That's why we have to be careful with helping and working in the ministry. It can be easy to become a busy body, and before you know God may be way somewhere else. In the beginning it was all God, but once you got all caught up, you don't really want God. He's on the back burner somewhere if there at all. In everything you do, you should always seek and God before you do anything,

Yes, I love to do God's work, but I love His presence more. I love the communion with Him. I love the intimacy with Him. Our relationship with our creator is the most important. He knows everything about you. He knows how to lead and guide you. It's going to be a lot of people on judgment day that think they're going to make it in according to their works, but not so. God said that He searches the heart of man and that the heart of man above all is deceitfully wicked.

Where are our motives? I don't want to miss the mark. I don't want when that day comes for Him to say, "DEPART FROM ME YE WORKERS OF INIQUITY." As for me and my household, WE SHALL SERVE THE LORD, IN JESUS' NAME AMEN, AMEN.

As I was sitting there, I felt like there was no life in me and the life that was there was wicked. I had generational issues that I was dealing with that need to be dealt with. I was so busy. I didn't have time to even sit still enough to wait on a word from Him if He were trying to speak me.

So, I began to pray, but I really didn't know where to start. I knew I was a woman of warfare and intercessory prayer, but right then I didn't even feel worthy enough to approach His throne. I knew one thing that moves Him is a sinner's prayer, a prayer of repentance. It gets His attention immediately, so I began there. I cried out, and that's when He revealed to me the dry bones in Ezekiel. I told him that He knows and only He knows. I continued to pray over myself and prophesy to myself. I spoke tendons and muscle and flesh over my body. Then I asked God to blow a fresh wind of His breath in my body from the north, the south, the east, and the west. I repented from not using the gifts that He entrusted me with. I told Him that I knew that He gave me the gift of healing, and I knew if I was really endowed with His power I could blow His breath from my body and people would be healed. So, I am empowered with His spirit. I will obey Him and walk in the spirit and in truth holy and acceptable before Him and His people.

I had very hard decisions to make right then in my life. I felt like I was in the valley of decisions, but I had to hear from God. I would not move until He told me. At the time, I felt like He told me to move, and that's what caused me to be in a rebellious state. You see, God will only tell you the same thing so many times. Then, He will allow you to go ahead and make your mistakes. If you are still disobedient, He will allow you to be in a reprobated state. We know we can't afford to be like that. That's a cold place. I almost felt like I could have been at the place of disobedience.

I am so blessed that God's grace and mercy that brought me out because if hadn't I wouldn't be able to minister to my beautiful Mrs. B, also known as mommy, I thank God for you. You were more precious than the finest jewel in the world. I thank you for carrying such a great destiny. God knew exactly what He was doing when He put me in your womb. For such a set time as this, He knew that I would bloom. I can hear the clock ticking: tick-tock, tick-tock, my ship is soon to dock. I remember when there was a time when I didn't feel like I could make it because my ship had taken such a great hit from the people of God and the cares of life were flooding me out. But when I talked to you, you knew exactly what to say to encourage me and brighten my day. Now, I can see my way.

It was such a challenge to watch my mom go through the pain and suffering that she went through. I sacrificed my business, my church ministry, and my kids to be there for my mom. I had to give up a lot in order for my mom to live longer. They call me the warden of the family. I don't like it, but somebody got to do it.

When my mom received the news that the Cancer was back, she tried to be strong. Normally, my dad was her strength. Because he was gone, God was her strength once she really plugged into Him.

One day, she had a temper throughout the whole house. She normally did everybody but me, but she gave it to me too, and I took it with a great love. It hurt, but I took it. Later, I was able to tell her how I felt and that she shouldn't give in to the enemy but give in to the things of God: positive, hope, and good energy. Evil and sickness can't dwell in all that good. So, she told me that I was the way I was because that's the way God created me to be from the beginning. She said "Don't change nothing." She said that I'm good for the people, for humanity. I didn't quite understand what she was saying, but I knew that it was big, especially the way God had been sending His people to prophesy and confirm some things in my life. He had been blowing my mind, and that was prophetically spoken over my life a couple of years ago.

Later that day, we decided that we would go to the beach and get away and let some things go. We went to the beach and were not able to release. They were ready to leave shortly after we got there. We stopped, got something to eat, and went on home. That's when it was on. My sister's best friend had called her, and they were talking and about fifteen minutes into their conversation, my name came up. She asked to speak to me. She wasn't saved or anything. She knew God in her early life, but she said that I was all in her brain, her mind. She kept calling my name saying, "Katrina, Katrina. God put you in my mind. I have been thinking about you. I need you to get to God. It's through you and only you." I began to glorify God, and she began to say, "Thank you, Jesus. Thank you, Jesus."

Then, she started began to speak as though she was speaking in tongues. She said, "That never happened to me before. What's happening to me? Why did my tongue twist like that?" She said that it was through me that God was going to save her, and He was going to use me as a guide. This young lady told me that God was going to reward me and that I will not want for nothing. Let me tell you that she just became a millionaire, and she also was saying that she never had nothing in common with me and that she is my sister's best friend. She said, "I just know you as her sister, but it is God that put you in my mind. He did it. Nobody but Him, and I know that it is a part of the plan of God."

She was obedient, and I pray that she will continue to be obedient in Jesus' name. She said she has to touch me and hug me that her life depended on it. She said she needed to do that to complete her.

Oh no, that sounds crazy. But God said that He was going to do some stuff like this. Some off the wall stuff. He told me last year that He was going to bless a remnant of people, a people that most people will look at them and ask why did He do that for them. He's doing it this year. His hands are wide open, ready to give to His specially selected people for such a time as this. You have to be ready. Get in your ready position. You have to be emptied out so He can pour in.

After we spoke, we called it a night. The next morning, the devil tried to stick his head in. When God is blessing, the devil is messing. My mom had to go to the hospital. She was having difficulty breathing. I know that God has the glory, and we had the victory. We would stand and fight. She was admitted again, and the fluid from the Cancer was building more frequently. The congestive heart failure didn't make it any better. My mom was so weak and out of breath, to say the least. With little movement, she was exhausted. So, my family and I went to the health food store and bought her some herbs that would treat her condition. I had been evaluating her for the last three days, and she didn't have high blood pressure because I took her off the blood pressure pills and replaced them with an herb. I did the same with her Cancer medication, heart medication, and cholesterol meds too.

When I checked her sputum, before she started taking the herbs, it looked very bad and infected. Three days later, I checked it, and it was a completely different color: yellowish. When the paramedics came, they checked all her vitals, and they were better than they had been in a while. That let me know that her body was accepting the herbs. I took her off most of her medicine and then eased her off the rest.

I did this same thing twelve years ago with the help of the Holy Spirit. It had worked then, and I believed God that it was going to work again, in Jesus' name. My mom didn't go back to the hospital due to the herbs. For the six weeks prior, give or take, she had been going to the hospital every ten days. That was not normal. We needed more time for the herbs to get in and do their job. The fluid needed to stop overbuilding, in Jesus' name.

God said there is no sickness or decease that is on the earth that He has not created an herb, a plant, a tree, or fruit that will heal you. He said that His people perish for a lack of knowledge. There was so much concerning my mom's situation. You see, God wasn't completely glorified from my mom's healing. He said that we are healed by the blood of the lamb and the words of our testimony. That means, it's a package deal; the Lamb's blood healed her, but she didn't tell her testimony like she should have.

Once she got better twelve years ago, she began to live contrary to the word of God. I mean she went to church when one of us took her, but she didn't have that intimate relationship with the Lord. As God gave it to me, I told it because her healing was linked to my testimony. I told God if He healed her that I would serve Him for the rest of my life: sold out. Her testimony was linked to her healing also.

As time went on, we started lacking on her herbs. Eventually, we stopped giving them to her. That was a big mistake. What we should have done was take it to the next level health wise because she had given up meat, white foods, and dairy products. There are certain foods and drinks that feed Cancer. I don't recommend just anyone to just try this with their loved ones. You first have to be led by God and study up on each herb and pray over them too.

At that point in my life, it was difficult to continue to write this book. Normally in situations like that, and even greater ones like losing my dad, I would have just stopped writing. It had taken me over ten years to birth this book, and I just couldn't stop at that point. I know that there are so many other people in the world just like me, maybe worse, maybe not. But, I decided to press and push this book out to give you hope and encouragement to fulfill your dreams and visions, no matter what obstacles come your way.

One day, I went down to moms. I went to the front to my sister's first. My sister had said my mom was down in spirit, so I went to the back house where my mom lived, and she was down. She told me, "Go on now. I don't feel like being bothered." It was not like her to treat me like that because I was her baby and plus I reminded her of my dad. But she told me something: all she had for me was some sugar. I asked her for a kiss, and she puckered her lips. We kissed, and I didn't bother her the rest of the day. The next day, she cursed out everybody including me. The same day, she repented. I guess she looked at me and said, "You the one responsible for taking my meat, so I'm gone let you have it too." The next day, she told me not to change anything about me, and that it was done before time, and that God did it in me for humanity. I was so amazed at her saying those words to me because I had never heard her speak like that. My mom spoke in very eloquent words.

A couple of days later, she told me that she loved me, and she said, "Thank you for everything." Coming from my mom that was a lot because there were a lot of times she could be a hot mess. I mean we didn't call her Queen B for nothing. She was the queen, and we were her servants, but she had gotten so much better, thank God.

As time moved on, my mom's body began to go through withdrawals from the sugar, the meats and sodas, and even a little liquor. Due to the withdrawals and the disease, she would get meaner and meaner. She would give the people that had been taking care of her a hard time by using a few bad words. I would jump in and say, "Mom, those are not appropriate words for you to speak." Then, she gave me a couple. Normally, she didn't curse at me. She gave me respect, but I guess she thought about. I was the one responsible for taking a lot of her goodies, but I would call them baddies.

I would let her have her moment. Then, I would go into her room and tell her that she really hurt my heart by the way she spoke. I told her, "I know that I'm your daughter, but I am also the woman of God. The bible says, 'touch not my anointed and do my prophets no harm'." I told her that I am both. I told her that just because I am her daughter that don't make her exempt, especially with the condition that she was in. I ministered to my mom because I was more concerned about her soul than her body. She repented to me and our family and then to God. He is just to forgive her through His mercy and grace. Thank you, Lord.

I told my mom that my greatest fear was not losing her but it was losing her to hell. As time went on, we were in the third week after my mom was on her herbs for about three weeks straight. She was getting stronger. She was breathing better, and she was taking less of the drugs prescribed through pharmaceuticals. Those are full of side effects. She had not gone to the hospital, and it had been over three weeks. Thank you, Lord. My sister asked her, "How do you feel, Mom?" She said,

"Good." So, my sister replied, "You feel good?" My mom replied, "I feel good, so good, so baby, I feel good."

Mom was still doing well. She did not have to go back to the hospital for about one month. I would say that it was up hill from there. To God be the glory. Thank you, Lord for your healing power and virtue. She just was not getting too much rest. She really missed my dad. I would sleep with her, and all through the night she would call his name. She seemed to be becoming delirious. The devil is a liar. I declared that she would be in good health and wealth and in her right mind to enjoy it, in Jesus' name.

At the end, I asked my mom, because she seemed to be doing well with the herbs and throughout the day time and in her spirit, if I could go home for a few days so that I could help take care of Jr. with school and all being because he was really struggling in his senior year. Also, I had to get more work done to get the book finished on time and try to raise the money for the printing of the book and the book release party. Also, I needed to grieve just a little about losing my dad.

So as you can see, I had four major issues that I was dealing with at one time, but to God be the glory. I knew He would not put no more on me than I could bear. So, I went home, and I was up there for about three days. I was only checking in with my sister and my mom's caretaker concerning my mom. They said she wasn't doing too good. They said the fluid seemed like it was back. I told them I would be on my way as soon as I could get someone to take me.

The next day, I received a call from my mom, and she didn't sound good. It was very difficult for her to breath, but she wanted to talk to me. That was big because Mom didn't waste her time talking on the phone to nobody. She was just telling me that the hospice people had brought her a new bed and that it was small. I replied, "Are you saying it's not enough room for me?" She said, "No," and in my head, I said, "Yea right." She began to tell me that she missed me and that I had been gone too long. I told her the same. She said, "So you know what to do." I told her, "I'm already on it. I'll be there tonight or tomorrow."

That Sunday morning, before I went out there, our family was having a healing and deliverance service. She really wanted to go, but she was too weak and in too much pain. So, I spoke with her on the phone and the Holy Spirit had me to address her about a deep issue that had been eating at her for many years. The bitterness had set in deeply.

You see, the family came out with those old family secrets saying that my dad had had sex with my mom's first cousin, and she had a baby boy. But, we didn't hear about it until we were grown. I believe my mom couldn't stand her cousin and her son and was pretty hurt and mad at my dad. I asked her, "How do you feel about your cousin today, Mom. Are you still mad at her?" She told me no, and then I asked her, "Are you still angry with your husband?" She said, "No," and then I asked her about the child, but he's grown now. She said, "No, I'm not bad at no one anymore." I told her that D loves her and he was innocent and a victim. She said she loves him too. When I told my sister, she told me that Mom spoke with her and told her that she forgave my dad because for one she said, "I have done some things I'm not proud of and he forgave me." To God be the glory.

So, I got down there later that day after taking my daughter to a healing and deliverance service that God had set up just for us because we couldn't make it down the hill. God did it up the hill for us right at my old church. To God be the glory. Right after church, we went down the hill to see my mom. When I got there, I saw that she was weak and not doing well at all. I told them she needed to go to the hospital, but they said that the home nurse was going to come and do some type of procedure but the people that were responsible for bringing the medical supplies forgot a piece. So, the nurse stayed there all night with my mom, and I slept in the front house with my sister.

As soon as day break came, I thanked God for waking us up, and my mom was on my heart and mind. So, I got up and did a few things for my granddaughter. Then I went to the back house where my mom lived, and I saw that she was uneasy. That was when I found out they didn't do what they were supposed to do. Then, they had the audacity to tell us not to call the paramedics. They were not going to have no one there until one or two, and I said, "The devil is a lie."

Her caretaker asked her if she wanted to take a bath, and she said, "Yes." My mom did not play with having an odor at all. So, we began to get her up and ready for her bath. She said, "No, not right now. I don't feel like it." She forced herself to lay back. At that point, I told Sally, "Let's do it her way." I began to clean my mom, and I watched how gently Sally washed her face like she was a newborn baby. She finally got it, but it couldn't have been a better time. I continued to clean her, and when I began to wash her poo nanny, she said, "Wash it good," because it was irritating her a little. I began to detail clean it as if she was a little baby. I remember when my mom was sick earlier and we would put her in the tub, she would allow me to clean every part of her body. But when it came to her intimate part, she would always put her hands out for me to hand her the towel letting me know that she had it from that point on.

Shortly after I bathed her in the bed, she was still under distress. I didn't feel comfortable at all about it, but at this time, my sister and the doctors had put Mom on the hospice program. So, they were waiting on the nurse who was taking forever. It was already enough that they left an important part of the equipment that they needed for a procedure that they needed to do on my mom through the night. So, there we were waiting, and I saw my mom getting weaker and weaker. My mom was so miserable, and I couldn't take it. I told them we were not going to sit there and let Mom die by waiting on hospice, so I made the call. I began to have my mom pray the sinner's prayer and ask God to come into her heart and to save her. She did, and as she finished her prayer, the paramedic came; they rushed her to the hospital, but not without me.

My sister was sitting with her while I was getting ready to go with her, and as my sister was coming out, my mom called for her oldest son Bobby. I jumped in the back with Mom. We had to pull off and get her to the hospital. I've ridden with her before, and the guy that was working on her was very familiar about Mom's condition. Her heart rate kept dropping, going up a little, and then dropping drastically. He told me that her airway was closing, and she couldn't get any oxygen. She was very weak, so I just prayed God's word.

At that point, he was about to intubate her, and I remember her saying she didn't want to be intubated. I thought she wasn't in her right state of mind. I told the guy what was going on, but he knew I wanted him to do whatever he could do to help my mom. He told me, "If her heart drops one more time, this is what I want you to do." He told me to help hold her neck, but her heart rate didn't drop before we arrived to the hospital. All I could do was pray and hold my mom's hand and talk to her.

We finally made it to the hospital, and the doctor had it set up to intubate her, but he asked me if the doctor had an order not to resuscitate. I said, "No, I don't think so." I did remember us having a meeting with the doctor and my mom, and she told the doctor that she didn't want to be put on a ventilator. I said, "Mom, you are a fighter. Can you at least let them know you want to be resuscitated?" She said okay, but we didn't understand what my mom was saying. I thought she was being influenced by the doctor because he spoke to her when we weren't with her.

At that point when she went into the emergency room, everything was going so fast. Before I knew it, I gave the permission to intubate her. I felt like I wanted them to do all they could do to save her, and if it didn't work, it was meant for her to go. They did try really hard to save her, but God said differently. My mom tried to hold on as long as she could, but she wanted to be with my dad. She was miserable without him.

When I would sleep with her all through the night, she would cry out calling his name Robert, Robert, Robert. They were together for fifty years, and now they are together for eternal years. To God be the glory.

I never thought my subtitle would cost me so much when God gave it to me a few months ago. I thought I had gone through enough pain in my past, but the Lord said not so. You will go through much for my name sake. There is a body of people that's about to come in, and it's going to take testimonies like mine to be able to minister to them. It's going to take so much more than what's going on now. I'm not afraid to tell it. The main point is that God will be glorified in what my family and I went through.

I mean, Satan has been so mad at us. It don't make no kind of sense. You see, he didn't get any victory out of my dad's or mom's death. Was I hurting? Yes, I was to the core. Did I stop and get depressed and die? Not so. My work was not done. I started this book twelve years ago, and I had picked it up and put it down. I had been through a lot of stressful situations that pretty much forced me to stop writing. We only get one mom, and for me, I only had one dad. I lost them both within five months. I just knew that I would be able to take a bereavement break, sick leave, or maybe I would just crawl up in a corner and not come out.

Somebody say: **But God! But God!**

Chapter Twelve

Walking into My Destiny

When I asked God if I could take a break, He told me, "No." He said to keep moving forward. NO BREAK! NO PITTY PARTY! He told me I used up all my time, and it was a part of the plan to continue to push. All I said was, "Really, really?" I said, "Okay." I didn't think twice. Have I always been like that? Of course not. I just knew that quitting or prolonging was not an option. I found out later that if He had allowed me to take a break, I would have been somewhere in a corner completely broken down and out of my mind.

There I was in the midst of all type of stuff and people. I was really out of my comfort zone, physically and spiritually. I was in a foreign land, and then it happened. The spirit of Ezekiel came upon me. God told me that He wanted to be so glorified through me and my parents' deaths. He said that I couldn't even mourn in front of the people. I'm not just talking about friends and family that come by to pay their respects. I'm talking about my immediate family as well.

Everybody was drinking and smoking. All I could do was be quiet most of the time and speak when He told me to. I went into my sister's bedroom and found some worship music. I praised and worshipped Him. I had been through a lot in my life, but never like that. I remember, I used to do exhortations at church. I would minister to the people and tell them, "I dare you to praise Him in the midst of your pain, in the midst of your hurt. I dare you, even though you're going through, God is waiting on you to praise your way through. When we go through trials and tribulations, it don't have anything to do with God's praise. So, right now, give Him what's due. Before you know it, you would have praised your way through."

You know, when praise dropped in my spirit, I couldn't be a hypocrite. So, I began to praise Him and worship Him, as if nothing was wrong. I began to feel better and better lighter and lighter. My family would try to get in. They would take turns, but they were bound. It's going to take a real miracle, but that's nothing. My God got it. One minute, I was ministering to my aunty, the way I could. I told her I would be glad when she started preaching because whenever she came to the family gatherings, she was the loudest, the life of the party. She never stopped. She went full force. She was always the last man standing, and she's one of the oldest.

I told her, "God could really use you. All you got to do is start talking for Him." This same aunty came over the next day or two, and she began picking on me. I was having a kind of rough day, but I was still just minding my business. I had already told her that she needs to learn how to talk to people and know what not to say to certain family that comes around. She said, "I know. Ok." But, I guess it didn't apply to me.

Hear me out here please. I can't believe this. It was about a week and a half after my mom's death. This is her sister, and she decided to start in on me. I asked her nicely to leave it alone. Some of the family were telling her the same. We were all in the living room, and we were talking about what my mom was going to wear. She started to say, "Yea, make sure I'm in my sister's obituary because you didn't put me in my brother-in-laws." I kept telling her that it was an honest mistake. It wasn't personal, but she kept on and on. I told her we talked about this months ago. She kept on talking, and I told her that I didn't even put my dad's beautiful mom's picture in his obituary and that hurt me.

I felt bad, but I never did my dad's obituary before. It was hard. I just wanted to get it done and over. My dad's sister had happened to be there, and she told her, "It happens. A couple of years ago at my mom's funeral, I didn't realize until they were reading the obituary that I had forgot to put my oldest sister's name in it." But, my other aunty didn't pay any attention to what she was saying. She had a one-track mind. That is until I snapped. I started yelling and telling her that I am done with her. I said, "Don't ever ever talk to me again. I'm done."

My sister grabbed my aunt and took her outside to talk to her. It didn't take long at all because she knew she had gone too far, so she came in and leaned over me. She said she was sorry, and she said,

"You know I love you," but I really didn't know because love is an action word. No way should my mother's sister be standing up bashing her daughter about her dad's obituary. I told her what she was doing to me was like having a deep cut and somebody just poured alcohol or salt in it.

You're not going to believe this. Later that night, when another aunty by marriage was working on my mom's obituary, she was supposed to re-write it. We were going to send it in, but guess what she said? She said after all the drama she couldn't believe that my mom's sisters that wrote the obituary had forgot to put my grandmother's name in it. Yes, they honestly forgot their mother. How did that happen? An honest mistake.

When you're grieving for someone close, you're bound to make a mistake because you are dealing with all type of stuff in your mind. I will always have my mom in my heart; she will always be in my soul, and she will never leave my mind for the rest of time. I love you, Mommy.

My baby Latrina, my baby sister, my baby brother, my grandsons and their dad, and the rest of my mom's siblings and their kids arrived from Atlanta, Georgia. The Lord had already told me that I would be the one to preach my mom's funeral, and I believe my mom wouldn't have any other way. At this time, we are still trying to raise about ten thousand dollars because the insurance company would not honor her policy. They wanted to give us three thousand, but we won't settle. They're going to give it all up. They already disrespected my dad and only gave us only fifteen hundred dollars. What an insult. But God is so good. We put my dad away in style, and we were able to do the same for my mom with God's help. I haven't worked since my dad died because I needed to be there for my mom. I didn't want to leave her side, and she didn't want me to.

As it was getting real close to the time for the service, we still needed about three thousand dollars, so I told my family that I was going to go home for a couple of days and go back to work and try to help raise some money from all my loved ones. I sent a mass text through my phone explaining what was going on with our family, and all I could do was wait. I had no room for pride. I sent the text to my old Pain Sisters, my clients, our family members, and my Christian family. I didn't get no response, not even an explanation from them, no help from the family or response. But thank God for my Pain Sisters. They came through. They asked me what they needed to give, and they did just that. They came through with groceries and their support. A couple of my clients donated as well. I thank God for them. May He bless them back in return one hundred fold, in Jesus' name.

I would also ask God to bless those that didn't have to give and bless them deep in their hearts so that no deceit or wickedness or a lack of communication will not cause them or me to fall. By your stripes, we are healed, delivered and set free, in Jesus' name. Amen, Amen. We don't have any room in our hearts to harbor resentment, bad feelings, dislike or anger. We must be free. Jesus came to set the captives free and free indeed.

So, we came up with almost all the money, but a little. We had to pay for the obituary, and the cousin that was supposed to handle it for us couldn't because they wouldn't take a credit card payment. That was the night before. He was trying to help us plus his dad at the same time. It was his dad, my mom's brother that was going to handle that for us, but he was way in another city. So, it didn't happen the night before the service, so that left us to have to handle it the first thing in the morning.

So, I went over to my daughter's house to drop Latrina off to get her and her sons ready for the service. Out of nowhere, my old friend Big C walked up, and she gave me some other money that she said she was bringing. When she walked up, I was having a conversation with my uncle trying to figure out how we were going to get the cash from him way out in Orange County. He wasn't dressed or anything, so she very politely interrupted and said to me, "What do you need?" I told her, "$345." She said, "Miss Essie must have sent me right here right now. I have my car note money. Here you go."

I began to thank God right there. That wasn't the only thing He did. When my sister went to the mortuary to make a payment, I was on a conference call with them to see how much more we needed. We were still two thousand shy with the flowers included. That was after they eliminating two of the limos and one of the motorcycle escorts. But, before that meeting was over, God intervened. I spoke up and told the director, "Didn't you say that my auntie's pastor, who is also your pastor as well, was going to help us out?" She said, "Yes, he said when you guys came to whatever you could do." So, I told her, "We're at that point now. My sister is sick and weak. She is spitting up blood. This is too much. We haven't even been able to grieve or mourn because of worrying about money. I'm sad to say the owner of this establishment has been getting all of our business, so he should be able to cut us some slack." She said, "Ok, you guys. This is what I'm going to do. I'm going to handle it from here. I never did cancel your limos or the escorts. You have your original package, and don't worry about anything else for right now. Just bring me the money for the flowers next week." You talking about a relief! What a relief! Thank you, my Lord.

I am sharing this detailed, intimate part of my life to let those that don't have life insurance know that this would be a good time to get some. It's not a jinks or anything. It's being prepared. I used to feel like that before I lost my dad and mom. I would rather live a whole lifetime with insurance and be covered when I leave than live a short time and not be covered. My mom's policy was a couple of weeks premature, and we didn't feel like fighting for my dad's.

The day came, and I had to preach my mom's eulogy. I couldn't believe it. I knew it was not me, but it was the Holy Spirit that preached through me. As we drove, I looked back, and I knew we were going to be late for my mom's funeral. The Holy Spirit had let me know the day before. I guess so I wouldn't panic. My younger sister jumped in the limo with my brother's keys to his van, the one in the wheelchair. So, we had to go back to the house, which made us late but not really late. We were really on God's timing. Yes, we arrived at 11:12, another twelve. I know that's crazy.

When I walked in the church, I saw my Darlene. She was sitting exactly where she needed to be sitting. I needed to just see her there because the night before she called and told me she was having car trouble. So, it worked out. Thank God for Pastor Charles and Rosalind. They have really had my back. They gave me money, and they picked Darlene up and brought her to the funeral.

At the end of the day, my close saints had my back, my front and both of my sides. I really felt the prayers of the righteous. They availed much. It was your prayers that helped me to stay strong and lifted. Thank you for your obedience. To God be the glory. To top it off, I left my sermon all the way up the hill, but I had a little notebook with part of it on it. God is awesome. The night I was preparing my message, I didn't know why I had written my base part a while ago on my big black book. Then, I wrote my message on my black and white notebook. Then, I wrote it on my little notebook that I got from God's Woman Conference. That's the one I had to preach from, but I really had it all in me. So, it came out of my belly and my heart.

The one thing I didn't want to do was see my mom in the casket. I didn't want to stand by it, but Pastor Charles was right there every step of the way. I did it, and I made it. You see, I was obedient because it wasn't about me. It was and still is about God getting the glory. There were so many people that accepted Christ that day. It was amazing. God got the glory, and we got the victory. Oh devil, where is your sting? Jesus took the sting out of death. The devil is always trying to stick his head up. He was mad.

Can you believe my sister's kids started fighting right after the funeral in front of the church? What a shame. As much as God had done for us and been there for us. Look at this. I had to keep moving on. I went on to the cemetery, and they stayed behind. It was so devastating for my sister. She fell out in the middle of the streets and was almost hit. Thank God, she wasn't. I have experienced two major losses that I dreaded for a lifetime, and it happened in a five-month time frame.

Am I hurting? Yes. Does my heartache? Yes. Even as I was writing I was hurting. But I am not and was not devastated. I am still encouraged in the midst of everything. I know He won't put no more on me than I can bear. The baby girl said at the service and it's sticking in my head: we are going to be just fine. I would like to share a quote that has been famous in my life that I heard Pastor Wooten say. He said that the devil can't work without a body. Then, he just gave me a powerful strategy: if you're right-handed get your shoes and get a permanent marker. On your right shoe write 'shut' under one foot and 'up' under the other one. Do the opposite if you're left handed. And every time the devil tries to come against you and tell you what you can't do, you get up and every time you walk you are not only stepping on his head but you are telling him to 'shut up.' Every time you decide to get up, you really trample over him when you walk. So, keep moving forward toward your destiny.

When we made it home, the repast was awesome. We partied like my mom would like. But more hurt came. We found out that my daughter Latrina's kids' grandmother had died on the same day of my mom's burial. We shall stand and hold on to His unchanging, great big, mighty hand.

I buried my mom, and I continued to write until God said otherwise. I would go with the plan that God has set. I decided to run on and see what the outcome would be.

I know I haven't mentioned my fourth issue: my son was going through all of this during his last year of high school. I knew it was much but I didn't know how much it really affected him until he sat at the end of my bed and told me in so many words that he was giving up two weeks before graduation. I told him quitting is not an option. You see, he doesn't talk too much when he should and when he shouldn't talk too much he does. He had told me that there were some appreciation cards that they had him to fill out for the day of his graduation, and one out of the two of them was for his grandma.

So, I told him how to work it out, and I began to call and speak with his teacher and principle to see whatever we could do to help him so that he could walk because I told him and the principal that it's a part of God's plan for him to walk then and not later. So, they worked out a plan for him He had been giving us all a hard time. He wanted me to do it all. The way I felt at times if I could have, I probably would have. But that would not benefit him at all. I had already messed him up. He is so inconsiderate concerning my feelings. He has a one-track mind. If whatever you are doing don't fit in it, he's not doing it. He has his mind set. He is constantly wanting and wanting, but he don't want to give at all, not even to himself.

Seven days away from graduation, he was fighting me to the end as if I were his enemy. I told him, "I'm not your enemy. The enemy is using you against yourself to destroy yourself." A few minutes went by and before I knew it, he was up and on his feet ready to handle his business.

As I encouraged my son to move towards graduation, I often reflected back to times that I shared with my parents and things that had transpired over the last several months.

For instance, I thought about how my mom tried to hold on after my dad left, but she couldn't hold on any longer than five months. That was for a few reasons: one was because God told me that my mom wasn't going to be here too much longer because of how close she and my dad were. He told me that shortly after my dad passed.

I was spending some time with one of my close but not so close friends. She had a word from God, and I knew it was from Him. There was no doubt in mind. She said to me that I should spend as much time with my mom as I could. She told me to take pictures with her, take her places and love on her as much as I could. I knew it was real; it ministered to my heart. I had been guilty of not taking heed and procrastinating, but that time I took action. I had already been released from the ministry that I was connected and committed to. God used her in that area of my life as well. She was like Harriet Tubman. She helped me to come out of captivity. I want to take the time to give a great big thanks and God bless you for the part that you played in that area of my life and my family's life. Your obedience helped me and gave me the time I needed with my mom.

Like I was saying, I left the church, my business, and my son that was graduating from high school at the time, and I gave my mommy my undivided attention. If the woman of God had not told me what God told her, I would have even more regrets. God told me to prepare my mom, and that's what I did. While I was preparing my mom, He was preparing me. I was giving her herbs, and I had changed her diet but deep inside I knew she wasn't going to be around too long. I was hurting so bad in the inside. I didn't know what to do. All I could do was continue to speak life to her. It wasn't the Cancer that killed my mom; it was a broken heart and a set time. That's why I can't be mad. Mad? No. Hurt? Yes.

But, if I could change the time and have her here with me right now, I wouldn't do it. I would rather her go in His perfect timing instead of my time. I know my faith or prayers were not in vain because I was praying that God would heal my mom and for her to live. That's what He did according to His will and hers. She's completely healed. There will be no more sickness or death where she is. To God be the Glory.

My mom left here five months after my dad. It was in the fifth month on the eighth day of two thousand twelve. May is the fifth month of the year. The number five represents God's grace; it is sufficient; it's more than enough; it's exactly what you need. God don't make mistakes. I trusted Him in spite of the hurt and pain I was feeling inside. The number eight represents new, a new beginning, a new life in Christ Jesus, forgetting those things which are old and focusing on the new, taking off the old man and put on the new man. Best of all, when we leave this world, we will put on an immortal body that will never hurt or die again, but we got to live right. We got to turn our life over to Christ like He turned His over for us. He took off an immortal body and came down here and put on a mortal body and then died, so we can live. But He has to live in us to lead us and guide us. We can't do it with our own being; we must have Jesus. Twelve represents order. I believe this is most definitely His perfect time of order, God's order. He has allowed a lot of things to take place that shouldn't have, but for such a set time as this!!! God is setting order. Can't nobody do it like He can.

In the time of Sodom and Gomorrah, He had to destroy the land because of all the things that were happening, such as the people were building their own idols and worshipping, not to mention how there were so many of them that were having sexual intercourse with the same sex: male and male and female and female, but mostly male and male. The bible said that He created woman for man. That was and still is His master plan; anything other than that is an abomination to God.

Let it be recorded that I love everyone and so does God. It's the sin He can't stand. All sins are not an abomination to God. I'm still dealing with order, and I guess I'm addressing some things out of order like when He destroyed the earth by water in the days of Noah. The people were already messed up from their forefathers' sins, such as incest, murder and disobedience. God used Noah to warn and prepare the people for the flood, but they continued to do what they wanted to do, and they even laughed at the man of God. Noah did not allow the people to hinder nor stop him; he continued to build. He was focused and determined and motivated, but most of all he was obedient. God is searching for a vessel in this day and time that won't be afraid of what or how people look at you or what they think of you. Noah had a great assignment to accomplish, and I'm sure he was agonized but what if he would have stopped. Where would we be? Where would humanity be? The Holy Ghost just came over me.

I remember as I spoke earlier in the chapter when I said my mom told me I was for humanity. I had no idea what she was talking about, but I knew it was deep because my mom was deep. The calling on my life is for God's humanity. I am a peculiar person. I am an ambassador for Christ. He can trust me to get the job down. It was a set time for order back then, and God is the same God today that He was back then. He has been trying to allow His grace and mercy to buy us time, but time is running out. I believe we are getting closer and closer. We need to get in a place of sack cloth and ashes, fasting and praying without ceasing. It's time for a holy fast, a fast that's sanctified by God. It's a time to cry out, a time to weep and wail, a time to blow the trumpet, a time to repent, and a time to rend our hearts to God, our whole hearts to Him. He will answer us and show us compassion and mercy. Believe in God and His plan.

When He allowed my mom to pass from this life, I couldn't be mad. Sad, but not mad. I asked God if I could take a break, and He said, "No." He said we must stick with the plan. There is a set order. I had to continue and complete this chapter of my life in the order God said. Though I had lost my mom, I still had my son to deal with because it wasn't fair to him. I at least tried to do all I could do to help him in the end of his senior year. He had his prom, and I had no money at the time. We were still trying to raise money to bury my mom. They said at his school all the kids had to ride on the charter bus due to prom night accidents over the years. I spoke with his school, and they made special accommodations for us due to our situation. They allowed us to take him from L.A. since we were already there and that's where the prom was also.

I remember his family on the other side asking me if we could do the champagne party in L.A. before I spoke with the school. I told them I would try but after speaking with all these people to make it happen I was not going to have too much more in me, so I was going to really need their help. Well, I did my part, and they provided transportation to pick out his and his date's clothes. After that they couldn't do anything else. One of my nieces on his dad's side helped me as much as she could. But God worked it out anyway. That's what He specializes in: making the impossible possible. So everything worked out well: his prom and champagne party.

A couple of days later, it was time for his grad night, and God worked a miraculous miracle on our behalf then too. The time to see if he would be able to walk across the stage came, and it came fast and hard. By the last week of school, he was ten credits of geometry behind, and he had no motivation in him at all. He felt like giving up, but I gave him one last big push at the end of his school year. I told him, "You have been in school for twelve years of your life, and I know it hasn't been easy with losing both of your grandparents so close together, but you have come too far to give up right at the end of your first stepping stone." I told him not to allow the enemy to trick and trip him up by just laying there. "When you're so close to your victory, it's my job to push you. I know if my parents were here, I wouldn't even be having this conversation with you." I told him to give a great shout out to his grandparents.

Then, I turned away and walked out of his room. A little while later, I walked back by his room, and I saw him sitting up and getting ready to get up and continue to move forward. If he didn't get up on that day, he wouldn't have been able to walk at all because he was at a place where he only had four days to get a whole year's worth of math done. So, he went to school and began another task. He worked so hard. He didn't even think he had it in him. The whole school was helping him because we thought math wasn't his strong subject, but when we saw him complete and pass those ten credits within four days with a B average I beg to differ. I think he's awesome in math and every other subject that comes his way. They are now using his experience to help motivate the kids that can't really see their way to clear. They used what he accomplished to give some kids hope.

Major issue number four was conquered. He made it and graduated on time with honors. To God be the glory. I asked him two questions: the first was: "Who made all this possible? Who did it" He said, "God did." I told him not to forget it. I told him to always make sure God gets the glory. Then, I asked him who is the world's greatest pusher, and he said, "You, Mama." Congratulations, Son for accomplishing your first stepping stone of many. Keep on moving forward and don't allow the things of this life to deter you. You stay focused, determined, and motivated in your mind, body, and your soul. God will be glorified for such a set time as this, in Jesus' name. Amen.

I started my life story twelve years ago in 2000, and I'm finishing it in the year 2012. There comes a time for set order. God is a God of order; He established twelve months in a year. He choose twelve disciples, he choose twelve tribes of Judah and chose twelve men out of the twelve tribes. Twelve is even the number of governmental order.

Let me give you my number of order in my life. I was twelve years old when I was first molested, and it took twelve years later for me to tell it to help back my younger sister's story about the same predator. She also was twelve. It was twelve years ago when I left my home town. My son graduated in the year of twenty twelve. My first grandson, my first grandchild, just happened to be twelve in the year of twenty twelve. The man I married was the twelfth man that had me. It was twelve years ago when my mom was first diagnosed with Cancer, which caused me to sit down long enough to hear from God. At that point, He gave me a book to write, and it took me twelve years to birth it. I finished in the twelfth year. God, my mom and my family beat the devil down for twelve years while my mom was under attack with Cancer, and he still didn't get no victory. It was God that said it was time.

I decree and declare that every boy, every girl, every man, every woman, every victim and every predator I speak to through the reading of this book that you are healed, delivered, and set free. You are no longer in bondage or a slave to your predator or your past. We all know where we've been, but we have so far to go and grow. You have to go through to get much pain to produce much gain. Know this: the greater the press, the greater your anointing. Never give up and never give in. Living for Christ, you will win. The truth shall make you free.

Anthony May, Jr.- He made it!

SPIRITUAL TABLE OF CONTENTS

(These are the key scripture that helped to equip and sustain me throughout my journey.)

For I am persuaded, that neither death, nor life, nor angels, nor principalities, nor powers, nor things present, nor things to come, Nor height, nor depth, nor any other creature, shall be able to separate us from the love of God, which is in Christ Jesus our Lord.

Romans 8:38-39

And we know that all things work together for good to those who love God, to those who are the called according to *His* purpose.

Romans 8:28

For we do not wrestle against flesh and blood, but against principalities, against powers, against the rulers of the darkness of this age, against spiritual hosts of wickedness in the heavenly places.

Ephesians 6:12

For the weapons of our warfare are not carnal but mighty in God for pulling down strongholds, casting down arguments and every high thing that exalts itself against the knowledge of God, bringing every thought into captivity to the obedience of Christ, and being ready to punish all disobedience when your obedience is fulfilled.

2 Corinthians 10: 4-6

Forgetting those things which are behind and reaching forward to those things which are ahead, I press toward the goal for the prize of the upward call of God in Christ Jesus.

Philippians 3:13-14

"Come now, and let us reason together," Says the LORD, "Though your sins are like scarlet, They shall be as white as snow; Though they are red like crimson, They shall be as wool.

Isaiah 1:18

When the Day of Pentecost had fully come, they were all with one accord in one place.

Acts 2:1

Or do you not know that your body is the temple of the Holy Spirit *who is* in you, whom you have from God, and you are not your own? For you were bought at a price; therefore glorify God in your body and in your spirit, which are God's.

1 Corinthians 6:19-20

"Even now," declares the LORD,
"return to me with all your heart,
with fasting and weeping and mourning."
Rend your heart
and not your garments.
Return to the LORD your God,
for he is gracious and compassionate,
slow to anger and abounding in love,
and he relents from sending calamity.
Who knows? He may turn and relent
and leave behind a blessing —
grain offerings and drink offerings
for the LORD your God.
Blow the trumpet in Zion,
declare a holy fast,
call a sacred assembly.
Gather the people,
consecrate the assembly;
bring together the elders,

gather the children,
those nursing at the breast.
Let the bridegroom leave his room
and the bride her chamber.
Let the priests, who minister before the LORD,
weep between the portico and the altar.
Let them say, "Spare your people, LORD.
Do not make your inheritance an object of scorn,
a byword among the nations.
Why should they say among the peoples,
'Where is their God? '"
Then the LORD was jealous for his land
and took pity on his people.
The LORD replied to them:
"I am sending you grain, new wine and olive oil,
enough to satisfy you fully;
never again will I make you
an object of scorn to the nations.
"I will drive the northern horde far from you,
pushing it into a parched and barren land;
its eastern ranks will drown in the Dead Sea
and its western ranks in the Mediterranean Sea.
And its stench will go up;
its smell will rise."
Surely he has done great things!
Do not be afraid, land of Judah;
be glad and rejoice.
Surely the LORD has done great things!
Joel 2:12-21

Do not be afraid of their faces, For I am with you to deliver you," says the Lord.

Jeremiah 1:8

"And He said to me, "Son of man, can these bones live?" So I answered, "O Lord God, You know." Again He said to me, "Prophesy to these bones, and say to them, 'O dry bones, hear the word of the

Lord! Thus says the Lord God to these bones: "Surely I will cause breath to enter into you, and you shall live. I will put sinews on you and bring flesh upon you, cover you with skin and put breath in you; and you shall live. Then you shall know that I am the Lord."""

Ezekiel 37:3-6

The LORD is my shepherd; I shall not want.
He makes me to lie down in green pastures;
He leads me beside the still waters.
He restores my soul;
He leads me in the paths of righteousness For His name's sake.
Yea, though I walk through the valley of the shadow of death,
I will fear no evil; For You are with me;
Your rod and Your staff, they comfort me.
You prepare a table before me in the presence of my enemies;
You anoint my head with oil; My cup runs over.
Surely goodness and mercy shall follow me All the days of my life;
And I will dwell in the house of the LORD Forever.

Psalm 23

Our Father in heaven,
Hallowed be Your name.
Your kingdom come.
Your will be done
On earth as it is in heaven.
Give us this day our daily bread.
And forgive us our debts,
As we forgive our debtors.
And do not lead us into temptation,
But deliver us from the evil one.
For Yours is the kingdom and the power and the glory forever.
Amen.

Matthew 6:9-13

For God so loved the world that He gave His only begotten Son, that whoever believes in Him should not perish but have everlasting life.
17 For God did not send His Son into the world to condemn the world,
but that the world through Him might be saved.

John 3:16-17

"Will a man rob God?
Yet you have robbed Me!
But you say,
'In what way have we robbed You?'
In tithes and offerings.
You are cursed with a curse,
For you have robbed Me,
Even this whole nation.
Bring all the tithes into the storehouse,
That there may be food in My house,
And try Me now in this,"
Says the Lord of hosts,
"If I will not open for you the windows of heaven
And pour out for you such blessing
That there will not be room enough to receive it.

Malachi 3:8-10

Give, and it will be given to you: good measure, pressed down, shaken together, and running over will be put into your bosom. For with the same measure that you use, it will be measured back to you."

Luke 6:38

But the fruit of the Spirit is love, joy, peace, longsuffering, kindness, goodness, faithfulness, gentleness, self-control. Against such there is no law.

Galatians 5:22-23

Now to Abraham and his Seed were the promises made. He does not say, "And to seeds," as of many, but as of one, "And to your Seed," who is Christ.

Galatians 3:16

No weapon formed against you shall prosper, And every tongue which rises against you in judgment You shall condemn. This is the heritage of the servants of the LORD, And their righteousness is from Me," Says the LORD.

Isaiah 54:17

"For My yoke is easy and My burden is light."

Matthew 11:30

And above all things have fervent love for one another, for "love will cover a multitude of sins.

1 Peter 4:8

To console those who mourn in Zion, To give them beauty for ashes, The oil of joy for mourning, The garment of praise for the spirit of heaviness; That they may be called trees of righteousness, The planting of the LORD, that He may be glorified.

Isaiah 61:3

Honor your father and your mother, that your days may be long upon the land which the LORD your God is giving you.

Exodus 20:12

Jesus replied: "'Love the Lord your God with all your heart and with all your soul and with all your mind.' This is the first and greatest commandment.

Matthew 22:37-38

I, the LORD, search the heart, I test the mind, Even to give every man according to his ways, According to the fruit of his doings.

Jeremiah 17:10

For what will it profit a man if he gains the whole world, and loses his own soul?

Mark 8:36

Beloved, I pray that you may prosper in all things and be in health, just as your soul prospers.

3 John 1:2

For men will be lovers of themselves, lovers of money, boasters, proud, blasphemers, disobedient to parents, unthankful, unholy, unloving, unforgiving, slanderers, without self-control, brutal, despisers of good, traitors, headstrong, haughty, lovers of pleasure rather than lovers of God, having a form of godliness but denying its power. And from such people turn away!

2 Timothy 3:2-5

Now a woman, having a flow of blood for twelve years, who had spent all her livelihood on physicians and could not be healed by any, came from behind and touched the border of His garment. And immediately her flow of blood stopped.

Luke 8:43-44

For the wages of sin is death, but the gift of God is eternal life in Christ Jesus our Lord.

Romans 6:23

If my people, which are called by my name, shall humble themselves, and pray, and seek my face, and turn from their wicked ways; then will I hear from heaven, and will forgive their sin, and will heal their land.

2 Chronicles 7:14

The appearance of the wheels and their work was like unto the colour of a beryl: and they four had one likeness: and their appearance and their work was as it were a wheel in the middle of a wheel.

Ezekiel 1:16

And Jabez called on the God of Israel saying, "Oh, that You would bless me indeed, and enlarge my territory, that Your hand would be with me, and that You would keep me from evil, that I may not cause pain!" So God granted him what he requested.

1 Chronicles 4:10

In the beginning was the Word, and the Word was with God, and the Word was God.

John 1:1

Special Dedications

MY QUEEN, MY TULIP- Mommy, you were one of a kind. God knew exactly what He was doing when He created you. He had me in mind at that time. You had a quality of life that I have never seen, and most people that I have known could only dream. You were the most beautiful and precious person ever created. You shined in the darkest environment, and in your presence, most people were elated. You were a peculiar person, a woman of few words, but when you spoke, people didn't just listen, they heard. You were a small lady with a great big heart. God knew what He was doing from the very start. You taught me how to be a lady and up to this day, I will never stop being your baby. You suffered a lot before leaving this earth, but from your suffering I am about to give birth. Your life was not in vain. God will make sure all your seeds will proclaim Jesus Christ's name. We shall speak and be heard through generations to generations with great determination, motivation, inspiration and great anticipation. You lived a wild and radical life, but I'm so glad before you left here you met Jesus Christ. I will always love you, Mommy.

MY DADDY- Nothing you have taught me will be in vain. The time we've shared, the things you've taught me, and the places you've brought me will never ever be forgotten. It's a part of me because I'm a part of you. I remember the times when we went out to eat, the times you decorated our Christmas tree with money, the times you taught me that it is so much better to give than receive, and now that I've met Christ and have gotten so much older, I see now why you're better off in a giving position than receiving. I remember, the times you took me and taught me how to ride a horse. There was a certain way you kissed me on my forehead, both of my cheeks, my nose, and then my lips. Your kisses meant 'I love you very much.'

I remember the time when you had to cook for us and comb our hair. And, if my face wasn't clean by the time you got us to school, you cleaned it with a little bit of spit and your fingertip. I remember when you told me that I was too young to wear makeup and high heeled shoes. When my pants were too tight, you said that I was stopping my blood circulation and my breathing too.

I remember one Easter when I had on these high heeled shoes, and I was on my way out of the door. My dad caught me right at the door, and he asked me where I thought I was going with them high heeled shoes on. He told me to take them off. I said, "Everybody else is wearing them, even Crystal." He said, "Who Crystal? That girl don't got no business wearing them high heeled shoes. She too young and too heavy for them." I remember when I was a teenager, and I would sneak and go to a party in the projects or sometimes my mom would let me go. When my dad got home and found out, he would find the party and out of nowhere I would feel someone snatching me up from the back of my collar or the back of my pants and direct me out of the party. I didn't understand then, but now that I have children and grandchildren, I understand. You really do reap what you sow.

MY BIG SISSY- I have a lifetime of stories. If I told them all, this would be our life's autobiography. You have always been there for me even when I didn't see you there. I want to thank you for being the big sister that you have been. I want to start by telling you that I am so sorry for not clearly understanding all the things that I put you through, like the times when I would get out of my bed and had to sleep with you. I peed in your bed, and you would get in trouble. Thank you for time when you pulled me back and saved my life. In return, you got hit and wore a body cast for a year.

Thank you for being there with me when I fell, broke my nose and busted my whole face. I looked like a monster, and they put me in a dark room to wait for Mom and Dad. You waited right there with me. I'm sorry for being such a spoiled brat. I wanted everything you had, even when you had your first boy friend. I told because I wanted one too, but I was extremely too young. I'm sorry for not letting you know everything that was going on with me. I really didn't think you could handle it. I guess that's what Dad and I had in common- not thinking you could handle certain things. I beg to differ; you are a strong woman that has endured a lot. I have always loved and respected you, even when you were at your lowest and in waiting to see you at your highest. I am so very proud of you. You have done something that I have never seen in my life.

That's when you decided to give up drugs and pick up Christ. You have been holding on a mighty long time. I commend you. I would also like to ask you to forgive me for every hurtful word or thing that I have done to you. I did not mean to put the whole responsibility on you when it came to Mom and Dad, especially Dad. You endured something that I could not handle. That makes you strong and stronger. Nobody will have a chance to trample over you or pull the wool over your eyes. I love you Gin Gin. I pray that you can put the past behind you, so that it will not predict your future. There is so much more in this lifetime for us to do. Not only as natural sisters, but also supernatural sisters. We have a bond that nothing and nobody can come between. I thank God for who He has joined together, let no man put asunder. We will not be divided. We will stand tall in the spirit, and know that no weapon formed against us shall prosper, in Jesus' name. I love you Sissy, for the rest of our lives.

MY LITTLE SISTER WYNETTA has been through since she was in my mom's womb. I pray to God that He will give us all compassion and patience to deal with her. Most of all, I pray that He will heal her from the innermost parts of all hurt, pain and bitterness. My sister has taken a loss that I couldn't even imagine losing. She lost a child. My precious niece passed. That was the first great hurt and loss that was in our immediate family. I believe God allowed her to leave to help bring us back together, so we would and could be saved and help save many. My little sister also had a very special daughter, who was her first born. Due to infirmities in her body, she was not able to raise her. My little sister has been through so much with the Department of Children Services.

I pray your strength, Wynetta. I pray God's mercy and grace to be upon you. I don't know how it feels to walk in your shoes, so I won't judge you. All I can do is pray and be there for you. Stay strong and know that love covers a multitude. Ask God to mend your heart, so you will be able to love and be loved the way you deserve. Know there's nothing too hard for God. I love you little sister, the one who made me a big sister.

MY LITTLE BIG BROTHER- it seems like when he came into the world, he had a job. He has been working since he was a baby, from finding crates, wheels, baskets and turning them into go carts to making key charms out of potato chip bags to melting candy and making big candy. He did all of that to provide for his family, from his little brother and sisters to his nieces and nephews. He has always been a hustler. He used to make donuts out of biscuits and so much more. He was a provider. He was always into something. As he got older, he got involved in gangs. I didn't know the full extent. I just knew that God would put him on my heart a lot at one point.

One time, he used to have to a helicopter, and everything was at my sister Gina's house. She used to be so mad at him to where her last baby came out looking exactly like him. I remember I would tell him, "Slow down, brother." I would pray for him and tell him time after time. I tell you my little brother kept me on my knees and at the altar on his behalf. Once he started coming to my house, I could never really rest too good because I would be afraid for his life. I remember one early morning about five o'clock, I heard something go past like lightning. All I could think about was my little brother, and I jumped up.

Before I knew it, he was at my back door. He said, "Katrina." Before he could finish saying my name, I was at the door with no clothes on. I didn't know who or what was after him. I just knew I had to let my brother in not even thinking about who was behind him. I thank God he was alone because my kids and my new grandson were in the house sleeping. So, I got on him and told him again to please slow down. I had not been having good feelings at all about him.

So, a little while passed, and I received a call that he was shot. They rushed him to the hospital, and they said it was bad. When I got to the hospital, he was in surgery. When he came out, he came out paralyzed. He was in the Critical Care Department for months. He was in a coma as well. When he came to, he told me while he was asleep

God took him out of the hospital bed and took him to the scene of the shooting and showed him everything in slow motion from up high. He was looking down at everything, and God told him that He spared his life by rerouting the bullet that shot him from the left side of his back right where his heart is. God showed him where He made the bullet go through his spine instead and that spared his life, but it caused him not to be able to walk.

God showed me in a dream where my brother will walk again, but our healing is according to our faith and faith works. Recently, he was in the hospital with a very serious blood infection that almost took him out. The infection attacked his lungs and shut them down. He had to be on a ventilator, and his temperature was one hundred and five point nine. So, there we were once again at the hospital with my little brother fighting and struggling for his life. God began to deal with me, and I began to look in the spirit. I saw that my brother was dealing with the issue of blood in the physical realm, but God was trying to bring him to a place to where He can give him a spiritual blood transfusion throughout his body, so that he can be a part of the body of Christ.

We all could go for a blood transfusion, so we can have the DNA of Christ. I know my little brother has done some things in the streets and in our family, but God is a forgiving God. I believe it has taken some time, but he is hungry for God. He will walk in his rightful place and in the calling on his life. He is at a place now where he really knows God is real.

When he would come to visit, I would almost send him home naked because I would strip him of every bit of red he would have on. My sister told me when she moved from her house, she had a whole bag full of nothing but red clothing from when he had it cracking.

HEY MY MO-MO, MY KA-KA MY BABY SIS- You have been out of my life for a very long time. I want to take this time to let you know that I genuinely love you, and whatever I have done to show you anything differently, I'm sorry. You are a very strong and determined young lady. You know how to carry your own. You have shown so much love to our mom and dad. All your sacrifices, all the time you tried your best to be there for them was not in vain. You already know how crazy Daddy was about you. He stayed on me to make sure I spoke to and kept in touch with how you were doing. He really told me to make sure you handled your business. You know what I'm talking about. Let's make him proud. Let's be all that we can be as a family and as women of God. Stay strong. Be encouraged. Be motivated. Stay determined, and don't take no wooden nickels. Accept no less than the best because you are the best. Love you, baby girl- you and yours. Take it to a higher level.

BABY BOY- first and foremost, let me start with he is my mother's joy. I am so much older than he. So, it's not like we grew up together, but I had my share in helping raise him and changing plenty of diapers. He had it pretty rough with my dad. I feel like he always tried to prove himself. He was super hard headed. My dad would tell him to think with his head up top and not the one down below. My little brother always seemed like he had a problem with me. He acted like I never gave him the proper attention, and maybe he's right. I had time for other youngsters that were in my environment and in ministry, but I didn't give my little brother the time he deserved from me, which led him somewhere down the line to begin to experience different types of drugs at such a young age. That kind of messed him up; it made him do a lot of things I know he regrets.

I know somewhere down the line, he knew that I always loved him because every so often I would hit him up in the bathroom. We would pray and talk. He would express himself to me about how he felt like I just forgot about him and never really did nothing for him.

Well, let me tell you from my heart. There were some things that you did that hurt me and disappointed me. I had to take them up with God, but I love you sincerely baby brother. Stay strong and find God for yourself and don't let Him go. I decree and declare that you will not die prematurely, but you shall live and declare the works of the Lord Jesus Christ. Love always your big sis # 2.

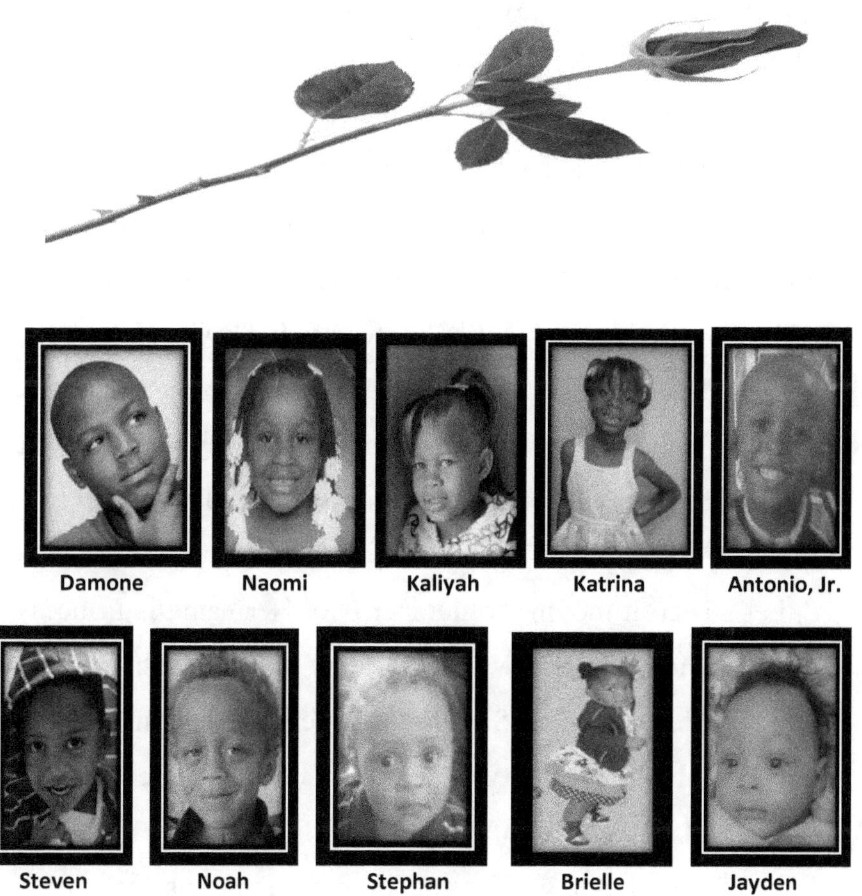

MY OFF SPRINGS: MY SEEDS' SEEDS- I thought having grandchildren would be dreadful, but after having actually experienced being a grandmother, I can't really think of the right word to describe my experience. So, I'm going to share several words and stories about my fantastic ten! Let me start with number one. He actually made me a grandma at the age of thirty-three. I know that's young, but in these days it's really not. I received a beautiful chunk of joy on Christmas day of 1999. I was so fascinated when I saw him. I knew it was another level of maturity that God was taking me to. So, I went right along with the flow.

Number one's name is Damone Young, Jr. He was born to my oldest daughter Evalina Dent and Damone Young, Sr. As Damone began to grow, he grew very close and attached to me due to certain special circumstances. Damone was raised in church. He loves God, and he loves his granny, better known as his Ga Ga. He always has my back. He has some issues, as we all do. One thing I know is, if you raise up a child in the way he should go, he may go astray, but when he gets older, he will return. So, I'm trusting and believing in the word of God.

Let's keep it moving to number two. Her name is Princess Naomi Merryweather. She also was born to my oldest daughter Evalina Dent and Paul Merryweather. She has been feisty every since she has been here. She also is a mighty woman of God. Her other name is Pastor Naomi, and at the drop of a hat, she will give you a sermon that will blow your mind. She will let you know when her pastor's hat is on and exactly when it comes off. She's awesome.

Here comes number three, right behind number two. They are so close. Together we call them twin cousins. Number three's name is Princess Kaliyah; she was born to my second child Temila Dent and Antonio Webster, Sr. She is a very intelligent and a quiet little girl. She is a watchman on the wall. I have watched her help her mom take care of their house and the kids. When she had too, she took care of her mom too. She also has a great appetite for God.

Let's slide to number four. When she was born, I knew there was a strong connection between us. That's why we named her after me: Katrina, not after the old me but the new and improved me. She was also born to Temila Dent and Antonio Webster, Sr. She is also Princess Katrina, but she wears many more hats. She is really sensitive to the things of God. She has a hunger for Him like I've never seen. She is a spiritual prayer warrior, a prophetic intercessor, and my armour bearer. She is still a child of course. I even see some of my old characteristics in her, but we have the victory over that too.

Let's keep it moving to number five, a number of grace. This is my Antonio, Jr. Yes, he also was born to Temila Dent and Antonio Webster, Sr. Antonio, better known as Tony or Pretty Tony, is truly a man and a good looking one at that. He also loves the Lord. I remember when I used to get in the spirit and pray and sing. He would imitate me by saying, "Halé, Jesus. Halé, Jesus." Whenever I would get up and get ready for church and he was anywhere around me, he was up and on the go too. I call him Pastor Tony. He is a mighty man of God, a mighty, mighty man of God. I would sing that song to him when he was a baby, and he is walking right into existence what I spoke. Thank you, Lord Jesus.

Ready or not, here comes Noah: grandchild number six. He is another mighty man of God. He loves to go to church, and he loves to praise God at any time. He is not ashamed of the gospel. He loves motor bikes, and he is a true mommy's boy. Every now and then he may trade her in for Granny. I love you, my Noah.

Here we are at grandchild number seven. I thought he was my completion for a while. His name is Steven Covyeow, Jr. He was born to Latrina Jackson and Steven Covyeow, Sr. Little Steven has the same anointing on his life as Stephen in the bible and even more. He is a man after God's own heart. I remember when I had lost my dad, and all I wanted to do was lay there and be depressed, but Steven began to start worshipping God right there in my bed. He began to lift his hands and wave them to God. When I saw and felt how he was reverencing God, I had to give God some praise and worship that I knew was due to Him. So, a special thanks little Steve for pushing me in the spirit when I didn't feel like pushing anymore. Thank you for encouraging me in the Lord.

Right after number seven quickly came number eight: Stephan Covyeow, to the same parents Latrina and Steven, Sr. Stephan is a very joyful baby who loves to eat. He's a good baby boy. I pray that he will also grow up in the ways of God.

They're coming fast. Then there came little Princess Breille Bailey. She was born to Evalina Dent and Brett Bailey. She's number nine, a number of manifestation. When she was born, there were a lot of things manifested in the natural and physical. She's a very humble baby. That is unless her food is late. She and her mom are very close, but it seems like as much as her mom has been bringing her to me, it seems like she wants her to be extra close to me. All is well, I guess her mom just wants her to get her time in with me, like all my other grands. To God be the glory.

Now, we come to the end of my first batch, where I come to a conclusion of the fantastic ten. But, I'm sure it's not the end. It's about to be another beginning. His name is Jayden. His name means grateful, and we are very grateful for him. When he was born to Temila Dent and Antonio Webster; he was their fifth child and her fifth C-section and my tenth grandchild, meaning God's grace is manifested. Even though the doctors didn't want her to have him because they said it was too dangerous, I prayed like crazy for him and my daughter to make it through. And they did. That's why we named him Jayden, which means grateful. He is only nine months, and every time I open my mouth to pray or praise, he tunes in and joins along. He also loves God.

I speak healing and deliverance over every one of my grandchildren, those that are here and those that will come. I release a blanket through generations to come through my bloodline. I speak that they shall do the work of the almighty living God and not the enemy. I decree and declare it in Jesus' name.

DARLENE- She is so very dear to me. I met her in 1999 at the Peace Treaty. At that time, I was already saved, but I was still going back to the hood. I was really trying to save the world at that time. You know how it is when you first get saved. You are on fire, and you want everybody else you know and come in contact with to catch on fire too. As time went on, she had happened to walk into a salon where I worked on Central Avenue. She said she wanted a short hair cut. Well, I knew I had met her. But, I didn't really remember where. I knew she was a strong and dominate woman. We didn't need no problems in the salon, so I usually didn't speak up and take the walk-ins because I was always busy. But for some reason, I spoke up and told her, "I'll do it." If anybody else would have tried to do her hair, it would not have been nice. I did her hair, and she was impressed. She continued to come, and in the process, we began to talk and share. I invited her to a program at my church because she told me that she sings. I knew that there was greatness in her, but she, like me, had really been through some things.

Oh wait! Did I tell you that she was from the opposite side from where I came from? She was from the gang that I couldn't stand the most. But God can do the impossible. Before I knew it, we were going out. She invited me to her house and to her job. At that time, Darlene was am exotic professional dancer, and let me tell you, she did it well like no other. God had so much more for us. As time went on, God was really dealing with me. You see, I was in a back-slidden state. I had started back drinking, but I knew that it was so much more for me to do.

As time went on, I made my way back to Christ. I would speak and dance, and she would sing. I saw her grow to be an amazing mother and woman of God. She has been a mother like I've never seen in my days. When I first met her, she had a very handsome son who was suffering with Sickle Cell. He had already had a major stroke and several blood transfusions and was still standing strong. As time went on, she got married and had my godson Jacob. Later, he also was diagnosed with Sickle Cell. A couple of years later, she had another fine boy who is the mighty man of God Jiher. He also was diagnosed with Sickle Cell.

She had to take them to the hospital every three weeks to get blood transfusions not to mention all the times they suffered with Sickle Cell crisis, which is an unbearable pain. Her husband was too weak. He couldn't man up at all. He had to go, so he bailed out leaving her to raise her three boys alone. Wait a minute. She was never alone. The Father, the Son, and the Holy Spirit have always been there for her in addition to her mom. Tin loves her baby and has always been there for her. Darlene really loves and has the utmost honor and respect for her mother, and I do as well. I love you, Tin for all your words of wisdom. Even though you changed my name to Patrina, I take it as a privilege for you to be here and call me Patrina. I thank God for extending your life, to God be the glory.

Darlene, you have been a friend like no other. I have been a friend to many but as an adult I had never had a friend. You have been there for me when my own family wouldn't. You have always seen me in the spirit and have never lost your cool with me, even though I've given you good reasons to do it. Having you as my friend brought things out of me that I didn't know were there, such as integrity. I appreciate the times you blessed me and the times away from home how you sacrificed your rest to hear my snoring. Thank you for the times when you put your problems to the side and helped me deal with mine. You never ever let me stop or give up. I love you girl, my sugar dumplin. My BFBSFL [BEST FRIEND BEST SISTER FOR LIFE].

BISHOP DR. LEON MARTIN AND HIS BEAUTIFUL WIFE DR. JACQUELINE MARTIN- and how could I forget their seed Pastor Carlos Martin and his beautiful wife First Lady Fatima Martin. I would like to thank you for recognizing who I am. I thank you for seeing gifts and callings in me that I didn't even know that I had. Thank you for all the times you loaned me your ears. I know it wasn't easy, but you did it. Your family has a special gift and that gift is a gift that is used to activate and cultivate gifts in others. Keep on allowing God to use you because only what you do for Christ will last. I love you.

PASTOR JO-JO (JOETHEL KEARNEY)- I love you so much, and I know that love could only be demonstrated through the love of Christ because it's that same love that you give back to me. His love is contagious when it comes to us. We make it a verb. It keeps moving and moving. We don't just speak it out of our mouths, but it speaks out of our hearts. Not just the way we treat each other, but it spreads on in whomever we come in contact with. You are beautiful from the inside out. I thank God He connected us, and He didn't do it just because. He did it for such a time as this. I speak encouragement to you. I speak life and life more abundantly to you. When the enemy comes in like a flood, God will raise up a standard on your behalf. Be of good courage, and stand, having done all stand. Love you, your soul-tied sister in Christ.

MY GIRL- I would like to extend a special thanks to my close friend and sister in Christ, Dr. Cassundra White-Elliott. You have not only been all that, but you have been a great inspiration to me. You have been a great push. You have been an awesome mentor. There were times when I wanted to give up, and it was you and your accomplishments that motivated me. When we first came into each others' lives, it was kind of bumpy and challenging. But, I thank God we didn't allow our own thoughts, feelings, and emotions hinder the great work and relationship that we have built over the years. I know I'm not all that easy to understand, but I would like to thank you for taking to time to speak, to hear, to see and to recognize the gifts and the call that's on my life. Thanks for the push, even when I didn't want to be pushed. May God do exceedingly and abundantly above all you can think or ask in your life and your ministry, in Jesus' name.

MR. AND MRS. DURHAM- I would like to give a special thanks and appreciation to both of you. You guys have been such a blessing in my life. For such as time as this, our relationship and the assignment that you guys completed were ordained by God, nobody but Him. I love and thank you for playing the most valuable and intense part of this journey, for every seed you've sown, for every late night and every early morning. I thank you so much. Only God knows how significant your assignment was in my life. If I may say a job well done, and may God continue to bless up and above, in Jesus' name. "I know sister Tranail, to God be the Glory."

JACKIE- I want you to know that I love you, and I appreciate everything you have sown into my life. I thank you for your obedience concerning our relationship. When I first met you, we knew that our relationship was much more valuable than just getting your hair done. God told me that He would also use me to be a blessing from the inside out, and that's exactly what He's doing. Don't ever give up on God or yourself. Continue to press on to see what the end is going to be. I have never met a lady like you; you are truly one of a kind, and I thank God for you. I love you so much. God bless you and yours. Know that all things work together for the good to those that love God and to those that are called according to His purpose. You love Him, and you are truly called. Now it's time to answer.

UNCLE GEORGE, MAMA BEV, RONDA, STEPHANIE, CHRISTINA, NIKKI, AYANA, JAMILLA, JEROME JR., AND LAST BUT NOT LEAST, MY BIG SISTER **REGINA**- I wish to extend a special gratitude of thanks to all of you for playing a special part in my life and in the development of this book and the book signing.

A Special Note to all Readers, Family, and Friends,

If the telling of my story offended you in any manner, just know it was not my intent. I told my story from my heart. If I had written it any other way, it would not have been *my* story.

ABOUT THE AUTHOR

Evangelist Katrina May has been saved for twenty years. Her name has not always been Evangelist Katrina May. Her name used to be Bad Seed, Baby Kay Kay, and a lot of other names that she chooses not to share. She is now called Mama, Granny, hair stylist, and armor bearer. She is a woman of many hats, and she wears them all with great integrity and appreciation- all to the glory of God. The enemy counted her out a long time ago. When she was five years old, he tried to kill her. She wasn't expected to live this long nor reach the accomplishments that she has reached.

She is the blessed owner of *Anointed Touch Hair Salon.* She has five beautiful children and ten beautiful grandchildren and more to come. What the devil meant for bad, God used it for her good. That's why she is proud to give you her new name: "Hurricane Katrina." May God's grace and His mercy be with us all!!!

www.ingramcontent.com/pod-product-compliance
Lightning Source LLC
LaVergne TN
LVHW020710110826
845149LV00012B/2193